THE ELEMENTS OF
GRAMMAR FOR WRITERS

THE ELEMENTS OF GRAMMAR FOR WRITERS

Robert Funk
EASTERN ILLINOIS UNIVERSITY

Elizabeth McMahan
ILLINOIS STATE UNIVERSITY

Susan Day
ILLINOIS STATE UNIVERSITY

MACMILLAN PUBLISHING COMPANY
New York

COLLIER MACMILLAN CANADA
Toronto

MAXWELL MACMILLAN INTERNATIONAL
New York   Oxford   Singapore   Sydney

Editor: D. Anthony English
Production Supervisor: Katherine Mara Evancie
Production Manager: Richard C. Fischer
Text and Cover Designer: Jane Edelstein

This book was set in Electra by Publication Services,
and printed and bound by Quinn-Woodbine Incorporated.
The cover was printed by Phoenix Color Corporation.

Macmillan Publishing Company
866 Third Avenue, New York, New York 10022

Collier Macmillan Canada, Inc.
1200 Eglinton Avenue East,
Suite 200
Don Mills, Ontario M3C 3N1

Library of Congress Cataloging-in-Publication Data

Funk, Robert.
  The elements of grammar for writers / Robert Funk, Elizabeth McMahan,
Susan Day.
      p.   cm.
   ISBN 0-02-340141-9
   1. English language—Rhetoric.   2. English language—Grammar—
I. McMahan, Elizabeth.   II. Day, Susan.   III. Title.
PE1408.F84   1981
428.2—dc20   90-34531
                    CIP

Printing: 1 2 3 4 5 6 7   Year: 1 2 3 4 5 6 7

Preface

Many good writers do not have a conscious knowledge of English grammar. They long ago internalized the rules governing the language and could not explain the system if they were paid to. But because they know these rules on an unconscious level, they can write accurately and effectively. Other people have had instruction in diagramming sentences and labeling parts of speech, but they feel insecure about applying their grammatical knowledge to their own writing. This book presents the fundamental concepts of grammar that will enable writers to compose and revise with confidence and intelligence.

Memorizing rules and analyzing sentences have little direct effect on writing skills. Writers must come to understand grammar in the context of their own composing processes. Our experience as teachers and writers has shown us that combining a knowledge of grammatical concepts with practice and instruction in writing will improve fluency and ensure correctness. Many writers need an understanding of grammar and grammatical terms to identify recurring problems and eliminate them from their writing. This text will give such writers a conscious understanding of the principles involved in producing and controlling the structures and conventions of English.

We offer clear, easy-to-understand explanations of the elements of grammar, provide numerous examples, and encourage writers to analyze and revise their own sentences according to the rules we illustrate. The "Usage Notes" give more detail about key concepts, and the "Writing Tips" show how grammatical knowledge applies to specific writing contexts. Used as a reference work in composition courses, writing workshops, offices, and tutorial programs, this handy guide to English grammar will permit writers to think and talk about their writing with assurance and understanding.

So many people have contributed to the design and substance of this book that we cannot possibly mention them all. But we would like to thank Tony English, Linda Jones, and Katherine Evancie of Macmillan Publishing Company for their enduring support and wise suggestions. We are also indebted to the following reviewers for their comments and criticisms: Victoria Aarons, Trinity University; Vivian Brown, Laredo Junior College; Robert Di Yanni, Pace University; Casey Gilson, Broward Community College; Polly S. Glover, University of Tennessee at Martin; Edward A. Kline, University of Notre Dame; Helen Quinn, University of Wisconsin at Stout; and Raymond A. St. John, Bob Jones University. Finally, we would like to give special thanks to Bill, Danny, and David Lee, without whom we probably would not have bothered to finish.

R. F.
E. M.
S. D.

Contents

Chapter 2   Verbs   25

Chapter 4   Modifiers   61

Chapter 5   Punctuation   74

List of Focus Boxes

A Word About Grammar

Like most words, *grammar* has several meanings. In the study of writing, grammar usually refers to sentence structure, and this is the part of grammar that will concern us most in this book. To write clear and effective prose, you need to understand how sentences are formed, how sentence parts relate to one another, and how these parts can be moved around and combined. An understanding of sentence structure is also necessary for mastering the conventions of punctuation.

To many people, *grammar* also means correctness in speaking and writing. People who say "I seen David yesterday" or "Him and the boss done the job" are said to be using "bad grammar." However, sentences such as these are *not* ungrammatical; they are completely natural to some speakers of English. They are, however, errors in *usage* because they do not conform to the way educated speakers and writers use the language. People who say or write "I seen David yesterday" will not be misunderstood, but they will be communicating something more than the last sighting of David. To most people, those speakers/writers are labeling themselves as people who use "incorrect" English—who are uneducated, careless, or ignorant. Although few of us would condemn these qualities with a word as strong as *wrong*, we would all agree that being educated, careful, or smart is preferable.

If you detect a note of snobbishness in this discussion, you are right. Correct usage is frequently determined by the traditions set by educated users of the written language—who, for the last two thousand years or so, have been until recently predominantly rich, white, and male. Some of these traditions are properly challenged, and some usages change because a living language frequently remodels without consulting the landlord.

We want to help you make your choices about language intentional and informed choices. In this book, we tell you what most educated readers consider *right* and *wrong* (and, when we can, how serious most people consider the error). We show you the various ways that you can correctly phrase and punctuate your ideas—ways that you may not have thought about. If, like famous writers G. B. Shaw and Alice Munro, you then decide to eliminate the apostrophe completely from your writing, we hope that the wit and wisdom of what you say communicates that you are an individualist, not an ignoramus.

Chapter 1
Sentences and Sentence Boundaries

One of the most important skills a writer can have is the ability to compose clear, complete sentences. The **sentence**[1] is the basic unit of communication in all forms of English. Understanding the parts of a sentence, as well as knowing the accepted boundaries for written sentences, will help you to develop this skill. The term *sentence boundaries* refers to the ways in which beginnings and endings of sentences are marked in writing.

1.A WRITING COMPLETE SENTENCES

Almost everything you write in college classes and in the business world should be in complete sentences. To write complete sentences consistently and confidently, you need to know what a complete sentence is. And to know what a complete sentence is, you need to recognize the difference between **clauses** and **phrases**. Knowing this difference involves distinguishing between **subjects** and **verbs**. Does this explanation begin to remind you of Chinese boxes? Well, grammar works that way: you have to understand the smallest units before you can make sense of the more complex structures that affect style and correctness in writing.

---

[1] Terms that appear in **boldface type** are further defined in the Glossary of Grammatical Terms, beginning on page 112.

Focus 1.1

USAGE NOTE: WHAT IS SYNTAX?

- **Syntax** refers to the systematic arrangement of words and groups of words (**phrases** and **clauses**) into sentences. Understanding how words combine to form phrases, clauses, and sentences is the fundamental concern of grammar.
- In English a sentence is formed by two grammatical units: a **subject** (S) and a **predicate** (P):

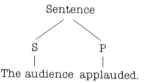

The audience applauded.

- The predicate is usually further divided into a **verb** (V) and a **completer** (C):

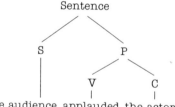

The audience applauded the actors.

- The verb is the center of this three-part structure; it expresses the action or state of being that the subject begins and the completer finishes. With most verbs, called **transitive verbs**, the action is carried from the subject to a completer, called a **direct object** (DO):

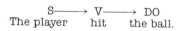

Focus 1.1 (continued)

- With **linking** or **being verbs**, a nonaction word links the subject with a completer called a **subjective complement** (SC), which either renames the subject or describes it:

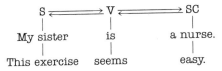

Except for a few sentences that do not have completers, the typical English sentence involves two important grammatical relationships: **predication**, the connection between subject and verb, and **complementation**, the connection between verb and completer. When these two relationships are combined

$$S \rightarrow V \rightarrow C$$

a thought, or sentence, becomes complete.

Finding Verbs

First, find the **verb**—the word that expresses the action in a **clause** or **sentence**. In a sentence involving no action, the verb conveys a state of being or acts as a link between the subject and whatever follows the verb. (**Being** and **linking verbs** are quite common: *seem, appear, become, am, is, was, were, will be, has been, have been, had been, should be, might be,* and so on.)

To find out which word is the verb, just change the time referred to. For example, if the statement is in the present, change it to refer to the past:

[present]   Juanita <u>leaves</u> for Hawaii today.
[past]   Juanita <u>left</u> for Hawaii yesterday.

The word you will change is the verb—in this case, *leaves*.

Finding Subjects

Once you have identified the verb, you can find the **subject** by putting *who* or *what* in front of the verb and turning the statement into a question. Let's use the same example:

Juanita <u>leaves</u> for Hawaii today.

[question]   Who <u>leaves</u> for Hawaii today?
[answer]   Juanita.

There you are! The subject is *Juanita*.

Resolving Complications

Unfortunately, this simple procedure for finding the subject does not work with all sentences, because sometimes the subject comes after the verb, as in these sentences:

There are ominous clouds just above the horizon.
Here is the latest weather report.
In which direction is the wind blowing?
Under the bed huddles our wimpy dog.

For the first two examples, you need to remember that *there* and *here* cannot be subjects because they are filler words (**expletives**), not nouns. Then go right ahead and ask yourself *who* or *what* about the verbs:

What <u>are</u>?	the <u>clouds</u> <u>are</u> ("just above the horizon" tells *where*, not *what*)
What <u>is</u>?	the <u>weather</u> <u>report</u> <u>is</u>
What <u>is</u> <u>blowing</u>?	the <u>wind</u> <u>is</u> <u>blowing</u>
What <u>huddles</u>?	our wimpy <u>dog</u> <u>huddles</u>

Recognizing Clauses

Once you are able to pick out subjects and verbs, you will be able to recognize clauses. A **clause** is a group of words having both a subject and a verb:

$$\overset{S}{\underline{Harold}}\ \overset{V}{\underline{ordered}}\ a\ cheeseburger.$$

Clauses can be **independent**—like the one above—and stand alone as complete sentences. Or they can be **dependent**—like the one below, which is not a complete sentence because its meaning is not complete:

$$After\ \overset{S}{\underline{Harold}}\ \overset{V}{\underline{ordered}}\ a\ cheeseburger.$$

See the difference? The word *after* leaves the meaning of that group of words in doubt, because the readers wonder what happened after Harold ordered his burger. To make that dependent clause into a complete sentence, you need to take out the word *after* or attach the whole thing to an independent clause:

$$After\ \overset{S}{\underline{Harold}}\ \overset{V}{\underline{ordered}}\ a\ cheeseburger,\ \overset{S}{\underline{he}}\ \overset{V}{\underline{changed}}\ his\ mind.$$

Those words, like *after*, that can turn a complete sentence into a **fragment** are called **subordinating words**, because they make clauses dependent (or subordinate). If you tend to write incomplete sentences, you will want to keep the list in Focus 1.2 handy when you compose and edit your writing.

Checking for Subordinating Words

As you edit the final draft of a paper, check each sentence that begins with a subordinating word to ensure that the entire meaning of the statement is complete. If a sentence seems to leave you up in the air, attach it either to the one before it or to the one after it:

[fragment] Although the train left at one.
[complete] Although the train left at one, we got to the station at twelve-thirty.
[complete] We got to the station at twelve-thirty, although the train left at one.

Focus 1.2

USEFUL LIST: COMMON SUBORDINATING WORDS		
after	only	unless
although	since	until
as, as if	so as	when
as far as	so that	whenever
because	still	whereas
before	that	which
if	though	while
	till	

[fragment]   Because I forgot our tickets.
[complete]   Because I forgot our tickets, we had to make a fast trip home.
[complete]   We had to make a fast trip home, because I forgot our tickets.

[fragment]   Which I richly deserved.
[complete]   Myrtle gave me a lecture, which I richly deserved.

Identifying Phrases

Because complete sentences need both a subject and a verb, you can end up with a fragment if you accidentally omit the *subject* (the thing you're talking about) or the *verb* (which tells what your subject is doing). Sometimes you may leave both out. This kind of fragment often occurs when you tack on an afterthought:

A warm and faithful friend.
Seventeen field goals in a single season.
By far the best in the movie.

Such fragments are easy to spot if you pay close attention as you edit. You can see that the meaning is not complete in any of those groups of words. Each is a **phrase**—a group of words that does not include both a subject and a verb. You can turn the phrases into sentences by adding the missing elements (usually found in the sentence before or after):

> Clyde is a trustworthy person, a warm and faithful friend.
> A warm and faithful friend, Clyde is a trustworthy person.

> Our place-kicker has an amazing record—seventeen field goals in a single season.
> Jose made seventeen field goals in a single season.

> Cher's performance was brilliant—by far the best in the movie.
> By far the best in the movie, Cher's performance was brilliant.

Telling Verbs from Verbals

Verbs (words expressing action or state of being) can also serve as other parts of speech, while still managing to look and sound like verbs. But once you are aware of this variety, you can spot the ones that are not **finite** (complete sentence) **verbs** fairly easily. The ones not functioning as verbs are called **verbals**. Here's how you can tell the difference.

Verbs that end in -en and -ing (and sometimes -ed) must have **helping verbs** (such as was, were, have, had, are, is) with them in order to be sentence verbs. Otherwise, those words ending in -ing and -en are verbals—verb forms that are acting like nouns, adjectives, or adverbs (see Focus 1.3). Verbals often produce unintended incomplete sentences:

[fragment]	<u>Stolen</u> while I was asleep.
[complete]	My stereo <u>was</u> <u>stolen</u> while I was asleep.

[fragment]	<u>Flying</u> in a soupy fog.
[complete]	The plane <u>was</u> <u>flying</u> in a soupy fog.
[complete]	Flying in a soupy fog <u>is</u> dangerous.

Focus 1.3

USAGE NOTE: WHEN IS A VERB NOT A VERB?

- Verbs that serve as the main verb in a sentence or clause are called **finite** (or "complete") **verbs**. Here are some examples:

Rick <u>went</u> to the game.
Rita <u>has</u> <u>been</u> <u>gone</u> several days.
Juanita <u>could</u> <u>have</u> <u>gone</u> early.

A **nonfinite** (or "unfinished") **verb** form cannot serve as a sentence verb. There are three basic forms of nonfinite verbs, also called **verbals**:

infinitive: to eat, to see, to refer
present participle: eating, seeing, referring
past participle: eaten, seen, referred

- If certain auxiliaries, or helping verbs, are used with the participle forms, the combinations become finite verbs:

be + present participle (progressive)

They <u>are</u> <u>eating</u> their dinner right now.
She <u>was</u> <u>referring</u> to the same article.

have + past participle (perfect tense)

They <u>have</u> <u>eaten</u> their dinner.
She <u>has</u> <u>referred</u> to that article before.

be + past participle (passive)

The pizza <u>was</u> <u>eaten</u> by the dog.
Both articles <u>were</u> <u>referred</u> to in the notes.

Focus 1.3 (continued)

> ■ Nonfinite verbs can combine with other words, such as modifiers, objects, and complements, to produce verbal phrases, which look like complete sentences but are really just parts of sentences (nouns, adjectives, or adverbs):
>
> **verbal phrases as nouns:**
>
> | | |
> |---|---|
> | [gerund] | Some students hate <u>writing research papers</u>. |
> | [infinitive] | <u>To become an American citizen</u> was his goal. |
>
> **verbal phrases as adjectives:**
>
> | | |
> |---|---|
> | [present participle] | <u>Sitting in the sun</u>, Mira feels happy. |
> | [past participle] | He ignored the man <u>seated by the window</u>. |
> | [infinitive] | A party is a great way <u>to end the semester</u>. |
>
> **verbal phrases as adverbs:**
>
> | | |
> |---|---|
> | [infinitive] | They worked hard <u>to improve their act</u>. |
> | [present participle] | She eats lunch <u>sitting at her desk</u>. |

Sometimes verbs ending in *-ed* also need a helping verb.

[fragment]	<u>Welcomed</u> by everyone at the party.
[complete]	Mavis <u>was</u> <u>welcomed</u> by everyone at the party.
[complete]	<u>Welcomed</u> by everyone at the party, Mavis <u>beamed</u> with delight.

Verb forms that begin with *to* are not sentence verbs either. They also are verbals, called **infinitives**.

[fragment]	Probably <u>to</u> <u>romp</u> in the snow.
[complete]	Lin <u>dashed</u> outside, probably to romp in the snow.

[complete]   Probably Lin <u>dashed</u> outside to romp in the
              snow.

Revising Fragments

If you have a problem with incomplete sentences, you need
to go through one extra revision, checking each sentence for
completeness. Once you learn to focus your attention on in-
dividual sentences, you will develop a sense for distinguishing
complete sentences from **fragments**.

The following examples will help you to begin cultivating
sentence sense. Each fragment is followed by two acceptable
versions to illustrate a few of your revising options.

[fragment]   Cracking and crunching under my feet.

[complete]   The $\overset{S}{\underline{ice}}$ suddenly $\overset{V}{\underline{began}}$ cracking and crunch-
              ing under my feet.

[complete]   Cracking and crunching under my feet, the $\overset{S}{\underline{ice}}$

              suddenly $\overset{V}{\underline{began}}$ to break.

[fragment]   Without a hint of warning.

[complete]   The $\overset{S}{\underline{ice}}$ $\overset{V}{\underline{began}}$ to break without a hint of
              warning.

[complete]   Without a hint of warning, the $\overset{S}{\underline{ice}}$ $\overset{V}{\underline{began}}$
              to break.

[fragment]   Too late to call for help.

[complete] $\overset{S}{\underline{I}}$ $\overset{V}{\underline{realized}}$ the danger too late to call for help.

[complete]   Too late to call for help, $\overset{S}{\underline{I}}$ $\overset{V}{\underline{realized}}$ the danger.

When you are revising your own writing, the fragments will
not stand out as clearly as our separate examples do. Read the
following paragraph, and see if you can find the fragments.

> In today's health-conscious society, many Americans hold myths about the proper role of vitamins. Although vitamins are essential for good health, excessive amounts are unneeded. And can be harmful. Millions of Americans take a multivitamin pill. Once a day, just to be sure. Then they stock up on vitamin C. When the cold season comes around.

How would you revise this paragraph to eliminate the fragments? There are three of them. Here is the way we rewrote the passage; see if you agree with our changes:

> In today's health-conscious society, many Americans hold myths about the proper role of vitamins. Although vitamins are essential for good health, excessive amounts are unneeded *and can be harmful. Once a day* millions of Americans take a multivitamin pill, *just to be sure*. Then, *when the cold season comes around*, they stock up on vitamin C.

1.B   SEPARATING SENTENCES CLEARLY

Sometimes complete sentences are joined together without the necessary punctuation to let the readers know where one sentence ends and another begins. You need to mark the boundaries of your sentences using the punctuation that readers expect, or you may create confusions like the ones discussed below.

Revising Fused Sentences

Fused sentences (sometimes called **run-on sentences**) occur if you neglect to put any punctuation between two complete sentences (that is, between two **independent clauses**):

[fused]   Marvin bounded into the room waving his tennis racket he smashed my Tiffany lamp to smithereens.

Your readers will be puzzled—perhaps even irritated—by being left to wonder where one sentence ends and the next begins. Because punctuation marks serve as guideposts for readers, you have, in effect, left out a crucial stop sign. Should the first sentence end after "room" or "tennis racket"? You, the writer, should make the decision.

Often the break between the two fused sentences will be easy to figure out:

[fused]   **Marvin bounded into the room he smashed my Tiffany lamp to smithereens, waving his tennis racket.**

But your readers may still be annoyed by having to backtrack and reread in order to discover where one sentence ends and the next begins. As you proofread, make sure that each sentence is correctly punctuated as a sentence:

[clearly marked]   **Marvin bounded into the room. He smashed my Tiffany lamp to smithereens, waving his tennis racket.**

The following fused sentences are followed by revisions that clear up the sentence boundary confusion:

[fused]   **The fir trees towered dark against the sky above them gleamed a pale, crescent moon.**
[clear]   **The fir trees towered dark against the sky; above them gleamed a pale, crescent moon.**
[clear]   **The fir trees towered dark against the sky. Above them gleamed a pale, crescent moon.**

[fused]   **Eating black-eyed peas on New Year's Day is a Southern tradition it's supposed to bring good luck.**
[clear]   **Eating black-eyed peas on New Year's Day is a Southern tradition: it's supposed to bring good luck.**

NOTE: The colon in the preceding example lets the reader know that the second sentence explains the first one.

[fused]   Sid carved a valentine heart out of a block of
           bitter chocolate then he gave it to his sister as
           a joke.
[clear]   Sid carved a valentine heart out of a block of
           bitter chocolate; then he gave it to his sister as a
           joke.
[clear]   Sid carved a valentine heart out of a block of
           bitter chocolate and gave it to his sister as a
           joke.

Revising Comma Splices

Standard English punctuation requires a mark stronger than
a comma—either a period or a semicolon—to show where one
sentence ends and the next begins. So, if you put two sentences
together with only a comma to separate them, you have made
what is variously called a **comma blunder,** a **comma fault,** or
a **comma splice.**

To clarify the confusion, you can simply replace the comma
with a period, a semicolon, or perhaps a colon. Or you can
add a **coordinating conjunction** to serve as a link between the
two sentences. Then, a comma is enough. The coordinating
conjunctions are these: *and, but, or, for, nor, yet, so.*

[comma splice]   The goats leaped gracefully down the rocky
                 slope, the faint tinkling of their bells
                 floated across the ravine.
[revised]   The goats leaped gracefully down the rocky
                 slope; the faint tinkling of their bells floated
                 across the ravine.

You can also revise a comma splice by making one of the
sentences into a **dependent clause** by adding a **subordinating
word** (see the list in Focus 1.2):

[revised]   <u>As</u> the goats leaped gracefully down the rocky
            slope, the faint tinkling of their bells floated
            across the ravine.
[revised]   The goats leaped gracefully down the rocky
            slope, <u>while</u> the faint tinkling of their bells
            floated across the ravine.

Using Conjunctive Adverbs Effectively

Sometimes comma splices occur because you mistake a **conjunctive adverb** for a coordinating conjunction. Conjunctive adverbs not only connect independent clauses but also modify the meaning of the sentence. Here is a list of the most commonly used conjunctive adverbs:

accordingly	furthermore	meanwhile	otherwise
also	however	moreover	similarly
anyway	incidentally	namely	then
besides	indeed	nevertheless	therefore
certainly	instead	next	thus
consequently	likewise	nonetheless	undoubtedly
finally			

Now, as you remember, it is fine to connect two sentences with a comma and a coordinating conjunction (*and, but, or, for, nor, yet, so*):

> Cecil hit the ski slopes, <u>but</u> Marcella headed straight for the hot tub.

You cannot, however, substitute a conjunctive adverb for a coordinator unless you change the comma to a semicolon (or a period); otherwise, you end up with a comma splice:

[comma splice]   Cecil hit the ski slopes, <u>however</u> Marcella headed straight for the hot tub.

Although conjunctive adverbs *appear* to connect just like coordinating conjunctions do, in reality they function more like adverbs than conjunctions, because they can be moved around in a sentence; thus they are not pure connectors. You could, for instance, place the *however* in the preceding example in a couple of places in the second sentence:

> Marcella, <u>however</u>, headed straight for the hot tub.
> Marcella headed straight for the hot tub, <u>however</u>.

You cannot move a coordinating conjunction in a similar way without producing nonsense:

> Marcella, <u>but</u>, headed straight for the hot tub.
> Marcella headed straight for the hot tub, <u>but</u>.

Because conjunctive adverbs are too numerous to remember easily, the sensible thing to do is to memorize the seven coordinating conjunctions:

and   but   or   for   nor   yet   so

Then you can be sure any other word that sounds as if it ought to be a pure connector really isn't. With all other words, you need to use a semicolon or a period to separate two complete sentences.

Here are several examples of comma splices followed by acceptable versions:

[comma splice]	Chas left the baking powder out of the biscuits, thus they came out as flat as hockey pucks.
[revised]	Chas left the baking powder out of the biscuits; thus they came out as flat as hockey pucks.
[comma splice]	Coughing and sneezing are among the first symptoms of a cold, also colds are most contagious in this early stage.
[revised]	Coughing and sneezing are among the first symptoms of a cold. Colds are also most contagious in this early stage.
[comma splice]	We were bored at the lecture, besides we wanted to be out in the warm sunshine.
[revised]	We were bored at the lecture; besides, we wanted to be out in the warm sunshine.

NOTE: Whether you put a comma *after* a conjunctive adverb at the beginning of an independent clause is optional. But if you make the conjunctive adverb interrupt the clause, then you ordinarily set it off with commas—one comma before and one after:

[revised]   We were bored at the lecture; we wanted, besides,
            to be out in the warm sunshine.

1.C ACHIEVING PARALLELISM

Parallel (or **balanced**) **structure** allows you to include a great deal of information in a sentence without losing your readers. A less skillful writer would probably have needed three or four separate sentences to cover all the ideas included in this statement about Americans' reactions to the turbulent 1960s:

> They don't know what to make of it all: of long
> hair and endless war, of their children deserting
> their country, of congestion on their highways
> and overflowing crowds in their national parks;
> of art that does not uplift and movies that do not
> reach conclusions; of politicians who come and go
> while problems plague and persist; of being lonely
> surrounded by people, and bored with so many
> possessions; of the failure of organizations to keep
> the air breathable, the water drinkable, and man
> peaceable; of being poor.
>
> —Bill Moyers, "Listening to America,"
> *Harper's,* December, 1970

After the opening independent clause ("They don't know what to make of it all"), every element that follows begins with the same word, *of*. But each element that follows is not parallel with the first one; the succeeding elements are balanced (similar in construction) in groups. Part of the effectiveness of this sentence stems from the variety of its parallel parts (see Focus 1.4).

Being able to make sentence parts parallel is a valuable skill. Even if you never attempt to compose a sentence as intricate as the one quoted above, you need to learn to balance fairly simple elements in order to become a competent writer.

Focus 1.4

PARALLEL STRUCTURE ILLUSTRATED

They don't know what to make of it all:

   of *long hair* and
      endless war,

   of *their children deserting their country,*

   of *congestion on their highways* and
      overflowing crowds in their national parks;

   of *art that does not uplift* and
      movies that do not reach conclusions;

   of *politicians who come and go* while
      problems plague and persist;

   of *being lonely surrounded by people,* and
      bored with so many possessions;

   of *the failure of organizations to keep the air breathable,*
                  the water drinkable,
            and *man peaceable;*

   of *being poor.*

Balancing Elements with Coordinating Conjunctions

You remember the coordinating conjunctions: *and, but, or, for, nor, yet, so.* The elements connected by these words should be balanced in structure. That is, the parts connected should both be clauses or both be phrases or both be single words:

[clauses] Melanie knew <u>that her new hat was too big</u> and <u>that it dwarfed her delicate features</u>.

[phrases]   She sported a hat with <u>a wide brim</u> and <u>a blue bow</u>.

[words]   Melanie never went out without <u>hat</u> or <u>gloves</u>.

You can most easily see the need for parallel structure by looking at an example that lacks it:

[not parallel]   Harold likes <u>skiing</u> and <u>to ice skate</u>.

Readers expect those underlined parts connected by *and* to be balanced, to sound more alike:

[parallel]   Harold likes <u>skiing</u> and <u>ice skating</u>.
[parallel]   Harold likes <u>to ski</u> and <u>to ice skate</u>.

Those connected elements need not be precisely parallel; you do not have to write *snow skiing* just because you choose to say *ice skating*. But you do want either two *-ing* words or two verb phrases beginning with *to*. Your ear will help you. Your sentences will sound better when they are balanced.

Here is a slightly more complicated example in which the elements connected by *and* are not balanced:

[not parallel]   Jo was ecstatic at <u>finishing her history paper</u> and <u>that she passed her French exam</u>.

You can improve that sentence in several ways. You can, for instance, make *pass* end in *-ing*, like *finishing*:

[parallel]   Jo was ecstatic at <u>finishing her history paper</u> and <u>passing her French exam</u>.

Or, if you prefer, you can revise by making *finish* end in *-ed*, liked *passed*:

[parallel]   Jo was ecstatic that she <u>finished her history paper</u> and <u>passed her French exam</u>.

Do not worry about keeping sentence elements parallel during your rough drafts. But when you begin revising to improve each sentence, pay attention to parts connected by *and, but, or, for, nor,* or *yet*. Try to get those parts fairly well balanced.

Balancing Elements in Series

When you write a series of words, phrases, or clauses, these elements also will need to be parallel. Items in series usually have the coordinating conjunctions replaced by commas, so they are treated the same as the elements discussed previously. Consider this fine sentence by Virginia Woolf:

> One cannot think well, love well, sleep well, if one has not dined well.

That sentence is automatically understood to mean

> One cannot think well [or] love well [or] sleep well, if one has not dined well.

To achieve a pleasing style, take care not to let items in a series slip out of parallel form, or you will lose the clarifying effect of a carefully balanced sentence.

[not parallel]   With proper priorities we should be able to
     help the poor,
     protect the environment,
     reducing crime, and
     balancing the budget.

The last two items in that series are not balanced and need to sound more like the first two, which do not end in *-ing*:

[parallel]   With proper priorities we should be able to
     help the poor,
     protect the environment,
     reduce crime, and
     balance the budget.

Or, you could revise the series so that the first two elements sound more like the *-ing* words in the last two items:

[parallel]   With proper priorities we should be capable of
              helping the poor,
              protecting the environment,
              reducing crime, and
              balancing the budget.

Balancing Elements with Correlative Conjunctions

Correlative conjunctions are those words that connect elements in pairs (*both/and, either/or, neither/nor, not only/but also*). As you would expect, these paired elements work best when they are parallel in structure; otherwise, your sentence will sound awkward:

[not parallel] You should neither exercise too long nor
                find that you haven't the time.
[parallel]   You should exercise neither too long nor
                too little.

[not parallel] Either the dog sleeps on the floor or it's the
                guest room for me.
[parallel]   Either the dog sleeps on the floor or I sleep
                in the guest room.

Balancing Elements in Comparisons

Whenever you set up a comparison or a contrast, make both elements parallel:

[not parallel] Running the marathon can be as exhilarating
                as the time I won the lottery.
[parallel]   Running the marathon can be as exhilarating
                as winning the lottery.

Focus 1.5

WRITING TIP: HOW CAN I SMOOTH OUT CHOPPY STYLE?

- When you compare your writing to the professional writing you read, you may feel that something is lacking in your style. Sometimes yours doesn't seem as vivid or compelling, sometimes not as telling in vocabulary, sometimes not as thoughtful—but sometimes it just doesn't sound as smooth. You may like your ideas and images, but they sound choppy, especially when read aloud.

Using Sentence Combining

- This process removes repetitive or useless phrases and shows the relationships between ideas and images. In sentence combining, you gather several choppy, related sentences and try to put them into a single, more sophisticated sentence. Here is one example of an introductory paragraph in choppy form:

> Like every teenager, I look back on my childhood. I think about early events in my life. Maybe they seem more magical than they really were. I don't know, but I do remember certain special memories. My cousins and I used to play dress-up in my grandmother's basement. She had old gowns there in a trunk. They were tattered and musty, but we loved playing dress-up in them.

This paragraph includes seven rather short sentences. It does have enticing images and is grammatically correct, but it lacks the flow of professional or natural-sounding prose. The writer should take a look at what can be left out and what can be combined. For example, here is one improvement:

> We loved playing dress-up in the tattered, musty old gowns in Grandma's trunk.

Focus 1.5 (continued)

And because the first sentence is overly obvious, it can be completely cut. Other ideas can be shortened and combined to produce a flowing paragraph. A smooth version of this introductory paragraph, written by student Antoinette Lewinski, includes only two sentences.

As I look back on my childhood, the recollections of early events in my life seem much more magical and enchanting than they probably really were. Even so, I still enjoy reminiscing about my cousins and me playing dress-up with the tattered, musty gowns we found in the trunk in my grandma's basement.

Chapter 2
Verbs

The **verb** is the heart of a sentence. Without a verb, a group of words does not really say anything. Verbs state, assert, imply, or express existence. They tell what the subject does or is. Successful writers pay close attention to both the form and the function of the verbs they use. Otherwise, their sentences can become imprecise, confused, or unacceptable to their readers.

2.A MANAGING VERBS

You have heard children say things like, "I taked too much," or "Wendy goed home already." These children have learned that past tense verbs in English usually end in -ed, but they have not yet discovered that certain verbs do not conform to the pattern.

Handling Irregular Verbs

As you know, **regular verbs** form the past tense and the past participle by adding -d or -ed:

Present	Past	Past participle
love	loved	loved
walk	walked	walked

The **past participle** is the form used with the **auxiliaries**, or **helping verbs**, *have* and *be*: "Pedro *was loved* by everyone"; "I *have jogged* three miles today."

But **irregular verbs** have different forms for the past tense and the past participle:

| take | took | taken |
| go | went | gone |

The most irregular is also the one most used—the verb *be*:

am/is/are   was/were   been

If you have not thoroughly learned the **principal parts** (the present, past, and past participle) for the most common irregular verbs, go over the list in Focus 2.1 to see if they are unfamiliar. Memorize the ones you don't already know.

Focus 2.1

USEFUL LIST: FREQUENTLY USED IRREGULAR VERBS

These are the fifteen most commonly used irregular verbs in English:

Present	Simple past	Past participle
begin	began	begun
break	broke	broken
choose	chose	chosen
drink	drank	drunk
give	gave	given
go, goes	went	gone
lay	laid	laid
lead	led	led
lie	lay	lain
run	ran	run
see	saw	seen
steal	stole	stolen
swim	swam	swum
throw	threw	thrown
wake	waked or woke	waked or woken

A more complete list of irregular verbs in English appears in Appendix A.

Or, if you find that too difficult, at least make a note of the ones you are unsure of so that you can look them up when you edit a piece of writing. (You will find a more comprehensive list of the principal parts of irregular verbs in Appendix A.)

Using Helping Verbs

Irregular verbs require the most attention when you combine them with **helping verbs** (also called **auxiliary verbs**). These helping verbs are used to indicate various shadings of time, both past and present:

> I <u>was</u> going, he <u>has</u> gone, she <u>is</u> going, they <u>were</u> going, we <u>might</u> go, I <u>should</u> <u>be</u> going, and so forth.

You are not likely to write, "They have went already." But what would you do with the verb *drink*? Would you write, "Agnes *has* recently *drank* only cola and fruit juice," or "Agnes *has drunk* only cola and fruit juice"? Here are a couple of tips to help you choose the right form every time:

1. Never use a helping verb with the simple past tense. (Of the principal parts *drink/drank/drunk*, the one in the middle is the simple past.)

[nonstandard]   Agnes <u>has</u> <u>drank</u> case after case of diet cola.
[standard]   Agnes <u>drank</u> case after case of diet cola.

2. Always use a helping verb with the past participle—when you want it to be a verb. (Of the three principal parts, the last one is the past participle.)

[nonstandard]   Agnes <u>drunk</u> enough diet cola to float a battleship.
[standard]   Agnes <u>has</u> <u>drunk</u> enough diet cola to float a battleship.

The past participle can be correctly used without a helping verb when you want it to serve as a modifier—as a *verbal*, not a verb:

[verbal]   **Agnes, <u>chosen</u> to make a commercial for diet cola,
            was delighted.**
[verb]   **Agnes <u>was</u> <u>chosen</u> to make a commercial for diet
            cola.**

Keeping Regular Verbs Regular

Only a small number of verbs, a hundred or so, are irregular, but some of them (for example, *go, come, do, eat, give, see,* and *take*) are verbs that we use the most. Indeed, sometimes writers are so accustomed to using irregular verbs that they try to turn some **regular** verbs into irregular ones, especially in the past tense:

[nonstandard]   **The veterinarian <u>spaded</u> Florynce's cat.**
[standard]   **The veterinarian <u>spayed</u> Florynce's cat.**

[nonstandard]   **We <u>drug</u> the piano up the stairs.**
[standard]   **We <u>dragged</u> the piano up the stairs.**

In the preceding examples, confusion exists between two regular verbs: using the past tense of the verb *spade* ("to dig with a spade") for the past of *spay* ("to remove the ovaries from a female animal"); using the present tense of the verb *drug* ("to administer drugs to") for the past of *drag* ("to pull across the ground"). Other regular verbs that sometimes cause trouble, especially in the past tense, are *drowned* (not *drownded*), *climbed* (not *clumb*), and *skinned* (not *skun*). The irregular past *snuck* is now acceptable in informal usage, but you should probably use *sneaked* in formal writing.

2.B   SORTING OUT SOUND-ALIKE VERBS

A few common verbs that sound alike cause considerable confusion for many writers and speakers: *lie/lay, sit/set,* and *rise/raise.* Should you write, "Luis decided <u>to lie</u> down for a nap," or "Luis decided <u>to lay</u> down for a nap"? You could dodge the problem by writing, "Luis decided to take a nap," but the distinction is not hard to keep straight if you remember the meaning of each verb and its principal parts:

Present	Past	Past participle	
lie	lay	lain	(to recline)
lay	laid	laid	(to put or place something)
sit	sat	sat	(to take a seat)
set	set	set	(to put or place something)
rise	rose	risen	(to go up, ascend)
raise	raised	raised	(to lift or increase something)

These tips will help you see the differences in the way these verbs are used:

1. The first verb in each pair (*lie, sit, rise*) does not take an object.

   Basil <u>has</u> just <u>lain</u> down on the couch.
   He <u>could</u> not <u>sit</u> up for another minute.
   He hopes that he <u>will</u> <u>rise</u> refreshed.

2. The second verb in each pair (*lay, set, raise*) will always take an object.

   object
   Sybil <u>has</u> firmly <u>laid</u> down <u>the law</u>.

   object
   She <u>set</u> down <u>a cup of tea</u> and bellowed at Basil.

   object
   She <u>raised</u> <u>a critical eyebrow</u> at Basil's ineptitude.

For a verb to "take an object" means that the verb describes an action that is performed on something or somebody else:

   object
   [with an object]   Norbert <u>laid</u> <u>a small mouse</u> at my feet.
   [with no object]   He then <u>lay</u> down and licked his paws.

object
[with an object]   Rosella <u>set</u> <u>her book</u> down in surprise.
[with no object]   She <u>sat</u> there staring at the poor mouse.

object
[with an object]   Rosella <u>raised</u> <u>her voice</u> to scold the cat.
[with no object]   The mouse <u>rose</u> unsteadily and crept away.

In other words, you can *lay* something down, but you cannot *lie* anything; you can *set* something down, but you cannot *sit* anything; you can *raise* something, but you cannot *rise* anything (see Focus 2.2, "What Is a Transitive Verb?").

These words all have other meanings which seldom cause trouble. Hens *set*; parents *set* rules; people *lie* about their age; some folks *raise* livestock. And nobody brags about getting *lain* last night.

Focus 2.2

USAGE NOTE: WHAT IS A TRANSITIVE VERB?

- If a verb needs a noun or pronoun to complete its meaning, it is a **transitive verb**. The term *transitive* comes from the idea that a person (represented by the subject) performs an action that affects some person or thing. In other words, there is a "transition" of action from the subject to some receiver of the action, called the **direct object** (DO):

  V   DO
  Roland <u>sharpened</u> <u>his pencil</u>.

  V   V   DO
  My roommate <u>has</u> <u>eaten</u> <u>all the strawberries</u>.

- One way to identify the direct object in a sentence is to ask the question *what* or *whom* after the verb:

  V   V   DO
  My cousin <u>is</u> <u>studying</u> (*what?*) <u>calculus</u>.

  V   DO
  Ramona <u>helped</u> (*whom?*) <u>her little brother</u>.

Focus 2.2 (continued)

- The direct object normally comes after the verb, except in some questions:

  $$\text{Which } \underset{\text{DO}}{\underline{\text{income tax form}}} \; \underset{\text{V}}{\underline{\text{should}}} \; \text{I} \; \underset{\text{V}}{\underline{\text{use}}}?$$

- To transform an **active voice** sentence into the **passive voice**, you take the direct object of the active sentence and make it the subject of the passive verb:

  [active]   They often $\underset{\text{V}}{\underline{\text{show}}}$ $\underset{\text{DO}}{\underline{\text{experimental programs}}}$ on PBS.

  [passive] $\underset{\text{Subj}}{\underline{\text{Experimental programs}}}$ $\underset{\text{V}}{\underline{\text{are}}}$ often $\underset{\text{V}}{\underline{\text{shown}}}$ on PBS.

- Some transitive verbs can have two objects: an **indirect object** (IO) followed by a direct object (DO). The indirect object refers to a person indirectly affected by the action; that person is the recipient of the direct object or benefits from it:

  Hector $\underset{\text{V}}{\underline{\text{gave}}}$ $\underset{\text{IO}}{\underline{\text{his son}}}$ $\underset{\text{DO}}{\underline{\text{a birthday present}}}$.

  The department store $\underset{\text{V}}{\underline{\text{allows}}}$ $\underset{\text{IO}}{\underline{\text{all senior citizens}}}$ $\underset{\text{DO}}{\underline{\text{a 20 percent discount}}}$.

2.C   MAKING SUBJECTS AND VERBS AGREE

One of the basic rules of English grammar holds that subjects and verbs must agree, meaning that a singular subject links with a singular verb and a plural subject with a plural verb:

An <u>aardvark</u> <u>is</u> a peculiar animal.

<u>Aardvarks</u> <u>are</u> peculiar animals.

Easy so far. But sometimes the choice of the appropriate verb can be complicated by the rest of the sentence. For instance, when using the *to be* verb (*am, was, been, is, are, were,* etc.), you make the verb agree with the *subject*, not with what follows:

<u>Bananas</u> <u>are</u> my favorite fruit.

My favorite <u>fruit</u> <u>is</u> bananas.

Compound Subjects

When the subjects are connected by *and* or *both . . . and,* the verb will be plural:

The <u>goose</u> and the <u>duck</u> <u>are racing</u> for the corn.

Both the <u>dog</u> and the <u>cat</u> <u>are sitting</u> on the veranda.

But when the subjects are connected with *or, nor, either . . . or,* or *neither . . . nor,* the verb should agree with the closest subject:

Neither the <u>ducks</u> nor the <u>goose</u> <u>likes</u>^{singular} corn that much.

Neither the <u>goose</u> nor the <u>ducks</u> <u>like</u>^{plural} corn that much.

Collective Nouns

Collective nouns, which name a group or a collection of people, usually are considered singular:

Theodore's <u>family</u> <u>is</u> quite small.

Our school <u>orchestra</u> <u>plays</u> extremely well.

The <u>audience</u> <u>was clapping</u> wildly.

Sometimes, if the members of the group are acting as individuals, a plural verb is used to indicate that the group is not considered a single unit:

> The curriculum committee disagree on every issue.
> Our old gang have gone their separate ways.

NOTE: Even when a plural verb is used correctly with a collective noun, as in the preceding examples, it often does not sound right. Some writers add a plural noun, such as *members*, to underscore the individuality that the sentence is supposed to convey:

> Some members of the curriculum committee disagree on every issue.
> All the friends in our old gang have gone their separate ways.

Several other collective nouns and pronouns (such as *rest, remainder, some, all, enough, number,* and *none*) can be either singular or plural, depending on how they are used:

> singular
> The rest of the movie is sloppy and sentimental.

> plural
> The rest of us are leaving.

> plural
> Some of the players are already on the bus.

> singular
> Some of the pizza has anchovies on it.

> plural
> All of the seats are taken.

> singular
> All of the pizza is stone cold by now.

With *none* the verb can be either singular or plural:[1]

> plural
> <u>None</u> of us <u>are</u> ever going to eat there again.
>
> singular
> <u>None</u> of us <u>is</u> sick today, at least.

When referring to *a number*, use the plural verb; when referring to *the number*, use a singular verb:

> plural   singular
> <u>A number</u> of students <u>are</u> ill; <u>the number</u> <u>is</u> larger
> every day.

The rest of the **indefinite pronouns** are singular and cause
little trouble with verbs: *anyone, something, any, anybody,
each, either, everybody, everyone, everything, neither, nobody,
no one, somebody, someone.*

> <u>Anyone</u> <u>is</u> allowed to attend.
> <u>Everything</u> <u>is</u> going wrong today.
> <u>Neither</u> of us <u>is</u> going to complain, though.
> <u>Somebody</u> <u>is</u> pounding on the door.

Expletives

It as an **expletive** (a filler word allowing for variety in sentence structure) never causes any problem with verb agreement, but *there* does. Just remember that *there* can never
function as the subject; the actual subject will follow the verb
in a sentence beginning with the expletive *there*:

> plural
> There <u>are</u> minor <u>accidents</u> at almost every corner.
>
> singular
> There <u>is</u> scarcely a <u>fender</u> in town left undented.

---

[1] The *American Heritage Dictionary*, 2d ed. (1985), points out that "for
centuries" *none* has been used "by the best writers as if it were a plural form,
taking both the plural verb and plural pronouns: *None of them have learned
their parts* must be considered an entirely acceptable variant of *None of them
has learned his part*" (page 470).

2.D KEEPING PREDICATION CLEAR

Faulty predication usually occurs with the commonly used <u>be</u> verb (*am, is, are, was, were, been, being*), which functions like an "equals" sign in mathematics:

Jocasta <u>is</u> my tennis partner.
Those lazy dogs <u>are</u> Bowser and Spot.

Jocasta and *tennis partner* are the same person; *Bowser* and *Spot* are the indolent dogs named in the subject. Thus, the subject "equals" the complement (whatever completes the verb).

But sometimes when the sentences are not that simple, the meaning can shift so that the subject and the **complement** are not the same thing:

[unclear]   Good grades and regular attendance are two of the typical problems that new students experience.

Good grades and *regular attendance* are not problems. The sentence needs to be totally revised.

[better]   Getting good grades and attending class regularly are typical problems for new students.

[better]   Getting good grades and attending class regularly can prove difficult for new students.

Sometimes predication can be imprecise without actually being illogical, as in this sentence:

[imprecise]   One essential point in the article was the part condemning terrorism.

The words in key positions are *point . . . was . . . part*, all words that convey little meaning. This revision says the same thing more forcefully in fewer words:

[better]   One essential point in the article condemned terrorism.

If you have problems with faulty predication, make a point of examining each sentence that uses the *to be* verb. Be sure that the subject and the complement refer to the same thing—and that what you say about the subject is meaningful. Your writing will usually gain precision if you replace the *to be* verb with a verb that does more than just connect the subject and the complement.

Here are a few more examples of sentences with unclear or imprecise predication, followed by revisions:

[unclear]   My first art gallery was a memorable experience.

[revised]   My first visit to an art gallery was a memorable experience.

[unclear]   The importance of eating properly is essential in maintaining good health.

[revised]   Eating properly is essential in maintaining good health.

[imprecise]   The plot of the movie is the intertwined lives of the characters.

[revised]   The plot of the movie follows the intertwined lives of the characters.

Clearing Up Mixed Constructions

Sometimes writers accidentally shift meaning in mid-statement and produce confusing sentences that are called **mixed constructions** (or **confused sentences**). Probably these structural mismatches occur because the writer begins a sentence one way, thinks ahead too rapidly or changes strategy, and ends up with an unsuitable result:

[mixed]   In times of high emotional excitement must be dealt with by soothing the cat.

The writer probably meant to express something like this:

[revised]   In times of high emotional excitement, I must speak soothingly to the cat.

But readers of the revised sentence still cannot tell just who is excited—the owner or the cat or both? The mixed construction may have occurred because the writer decided in mid-sentence to adopt a more formal stance and avoid using the pronoun *I*. If that was the intent, the sentence should have come out like one of these versions:

[revised] When a cat is in a highly emotional state, one should speak to it soothingly.

[revised] A cat in a highly emotional state should be spoken to soothingly.

A mixed construction poses a serious lapse in communication. You must train yourself to notice these linguistic accidents as you revise and proofread. Otherwise, they will seriously undermine your credibility as a writer.

The following examples of confused sentences show that sometimes the addition or omission of a single word can derail a sentence. The revisions illustrate some of the strategies for clearing up mixed constructions.

[mixed] Only by constant vigilance can save our constitutional rights.

[revised] Only constant vigilance can save our constitutional rights.

[revised] Only by constant vigilance can we save our constitutional rights.

[mixed] In his attempts to reach the steak caused the dog to fall off the stool.

[revised] In his attempts to reach the steak, the dog fell off the stool.

[revised] His attempts to reach the steak caused the dog to fall off the stool.

[mixed] Having stayed up half the night studying is not a good way to prepare for a test.

[revised] Staying up half the night to study is not a good way to prepare for a test.

[mixed]	Although Clyde loves bacon doesn't mean it's good for him.
[revised]	Although Clyde loves bacon, that doesn't mean it's good for him.
[revised]	The fact that Clyde loves bacon doesn't mean it's good for him.

2.E   USING TENSE CONSISTENTLY

The **tense** of a verb tells *when* the action or state of being occurs. Most people select tense without thinking much about it—except, perhaps, to decide initially whether to write in the present or past tense.

Focus 2.3

WRITING TIP: WHAT TENSE DO I USE FOR WRITING ABOUT LITERATURE AND FILM?

- Usually writers give little thought to choosing a tense. We write in present tense about things that are currently happening and in past tense about things that have already happened.

Using the Literary Present Tense

- But if you are writing about literature or film, you will probably want to use the present tense even though you may be referring to works written decades ago, authors long dead, and characters never alive. The use of present tense makes sense if you consider that the works, the authors, and the characters still live in our imaginations.

Adventures of Huckleberry Finn by Mark Twain <u>is</u> one of our greatest American novels.

Mark Twain <u>remains</u> our most famous American humorist, despite his deep and abiding cynicism.

Huck Finn <u>tells</u> fibs to get himself and Jim out of scrapes, yet honesty <u>is</u> one of his great virtues.

Focus 2.3 (continued)

Adjusting Tense When You Quote

■ If you are discussing a work written in past tense, you may need to change the tense in your quotations to make the quoted material consistent with the tense of your paper. You should enclose your tense changes in brackets, as we have done with the verb *stretch* in this example:

> By using positive visual imagery, Chopin indicates the affirmative nature of Edna's suicide. As Edna stands on the beach, naked "like some newborn creature," she sees "the water of the Gulf stretch[ing] out before her, gleaming with the million lights of the sun" (210).

In Chopin's novella, *The Awakening*, from which that quotation is taken, the verb is past tense—<u>stretched</u>. You may, of course, write literary papers in past tense if you prefer:

> In the character Edna Pontieller, Chopin <u>created</u> a woman ahead of her time.

■ **Just remember to be consistent**: choose present or past and stick with it.

The basic tenses in English are these:

Present	I play
Past	I played
Future	I will play
Present perfect[2]	I have played
Past perfect	I had played
Future perfect	I will have played

Sometimes, you will shift tense on purpose. For instance, if you are writing in present tense, you will shift to the past tense whenever you mention something that happened in the

[2] The perfect tenses indicate action already completed. See Appendix B for a fuller explanation of tenses, including the progressive forms.

past, or you will shift to the future tense when you mention something that is going to happen in the future:

> Although I regularly <u>play</u> first clarinet in the lo-
> cal symphony, last month I <u>played</u> with the college
> jazz group and next week <u>will</u> <u>play</u> with the Big Red
> Marching Machine.

And, if you are writing in the past tense, you will shift to past perfect when you mention something that happened even further in the past:

> I was glad that I <u>had</u> <u>played</u> in the marching band in
> high school.

But you do not want to change tenses needlessly. If you begin writing in past tense, do not shift into present tense without a reason:

[shift] The squirrel <u>twitched</u> its tail tantalizingly and <u>scampers</u> halfway down the trunk, while Teddy <u>was</u> <u>barking</u> in a frenzy and <u>races</u> around the tree.

[revised] The squirrel <u>twitched</u> its tail tantalizingly and <u>scampered</u> halfway down the trunk, while Teddy <u>barked</u> in a frenzy and <u>raced</u> around the tree.

Sometimes an unnecessary tense shift is caused by a typo. Because the letters s and d are side by side on the keyboard, a slip of the finger can cause a change in tense (<u>raced</u> can become <u>races</u> or <u>races</u> can become <u>raced</u>). Take care in proofreading to be sure that the tenses have not accidentally shifted on you.

2.F   USING ACTIVE AND PASSIVE VOICE

Verbs have two **voices**—**active** and **passive**. The active voice is used more frequently because it is usually more forceful and more economical. Passive verbs have an extra **auxiliary**:

some form of *be* followed by a **past participle**, as the following comparison shows:

Active voice	Passive voice
writes	is written
loved	was loved
are studying	are being studied
has planned	has been planned
will complete	will be completed
may question	may be questioned

Because passive verbs contain that additional auxiliary, they are wordier than active verbs and sometimes more difficult to understand:

[passive]   Living in a dorm room <u>can</u> <u>be</u> more easily <u>adjusted</u> to than living off campus.

[active]   Freshmen <u>can</u> <u>adjust</u> more easily to living in a dorm room than to living off campus.

The passive voice also provides a way of phrasing a sentence without saying who or what is responsible for the action expressed by the verb:

The crime <u>is</u> <u>being</u> <u>investigated</u>.
Your order <u>has</u> <u>been</u> <u>lost</u>.

These sentences do not reveal who is doing the investigating or who lost the order.

You will probably want to avoid unnecessary passive constructions and use the active voice whenever possible. But the passive is effective in some situations, particularly if the person performing the action is not known or is less important than the receiver of the action:

Martin <u>was</u> <u>wounded</u> in Vietnam.
More durable goods <u>are</u> <u>manufactured</u> in Chicago than in any other city in the country.
The streets <u>have</u> <u>been</u> <u>laid</u> out in a circular pattern.
Sherry <u>will</u> <u>be</u> <u>admitted</u> to the hospital tomorrow.

Chapter 3
Pronouns

Pronouns, as their name implies, stand for nouns. They also send out important grammatical signals, such as **number**, **case**, **person**, and **gender**. Used accurately, pronouns help a writer develop ideas and tie points together without using the same nouns again and again.

3.A CHOOSING THE CORRECT CASE OF PRONOUNS

Case is a holdover from Old English when all nouns, pronouns, and adjectives had inflectional endings to indicate their function in a sentence. Now only pronouns change form to show whether they are subjects, objects, or possessives. Nouns, for instance, remain the same whether used as subject or object:

[nouns]   <u>Juan</u> looks ravishing in that red running suit.
That red running suit looks ravishing on <u>Juan</u>.

But notice what happens if we use pronouns in those sentences:

[pronouns]   <u>He</u> looks ravishing in that red running suit.
That red running suit looks ravishing on <u>him</u>.

As you would expect, pronouns in the **subjective** (or nominative) **case** serve as *subjects*, those in the **objective case** serve as *objects*, and those in the **possessive** case show *possession* (see Focus 3.1 for a complete list). Choosing the correct pronoun comes naturally for most people—as long as there is only a single subject and a single object. But things get tricky when subjects and objects are compound.

Focus 3.1

USEFUL LIST: CASES OF PRONOUNS

Subjective	*Objective*	*Possessive*
I	me	my/mine
you	you	your/yours
he/she/it	him/her/it	his/her/hers/its
we	us	our/ours
they	them	their/theirs
who	whom	whose
whoever	whomever	

Using Pronouns with Compounds

Lots of people have trouble deciding which pronouns to choose if a sentence has two subjects or objects:

Bernice and (<u>I</u> or <u>me</u>?) barely caught the bus.
Bruno sat across the aisle from Bernice and (<u>I</u> or <u>me</u>?).

If your eyes glaze at the thought of identifying subjects and objects, you can forget it here. There is an easier way that is almost foolproof. All you have to do is this:

READ THE SENTENCE LEAVING OUT THE NOUN (LEAVE ONLY THE PRONOUN).

For instance, which would you write?

<u>Me</u> barely caught the bus.

or

<u>I</u> barely caught the bus.

Of course, you would choose:

[standard] I barely caught the bus.

Which would you write?

Bruno sat across from I.

or

Bruno sat across from me.

Naturally, you would select:

[standard] Bruno sat across from me.

Do not worry if the sentence doesn't sound quite right when you use this technique; the standard pronoun will still sound better than the nonstandard one. Consider this sentence:

Bernice and (I or me?) are taking the train next time.

Ask yourself which it should be:

Me are taking the train.

or

I are taking the train.

When you adjust the verb to agree with the subject, which is now singular, you get a standard sentence—"I am taking the train." Then try, "Me am taking the train," and you realize only someone under the age of three would be likely to choose that pronoun. So, the use of *I* is confirmed:

[standard] Bernice and I are taking the train next time.

Using Pronouns with Prepositions

Because the most common **prepositions** are short (*in, by, on, at, for*), many people forget that *between, beside, among,* *through*, and *underneath* are also prepositions. Be sure to use the objective case after all prepositions—long or short:

[standard]   I like a satin comforter <u>between</u> the cat and <u>me</u>.
[standard]   Roscoe wants the dog to sit <u>beside</u> <u>him</u> and Eloise.
[standard]   The prize will be divided <u>among</u> Rudy, Ringo, and <u>her</u>.

Substitution works here, too, if you need it. Drop the extra nouns and try both pronouns:

between <u>I</u> or between <u>me</u>?
beside <u>he</u>? or beside <u>him</u>?
among <u>she</u>? or among <u>her</u>?

None of those combinations will sound just right, but the second of each pair should still prove an easy choice.

Using Pronouns with Appositives

The same method—dropping out the noun to see which pronoun sounds better—works well with **appositives** (words that identify or rename another word). All you need to do is read the sentence without the word (or words) that the pronoun renames:

(<u>Us</u> or <u>we</u>?) students are going to evaluate the faculty.

Drop out the appositive, *students*. Which would you write?

<u>Us</u> are going to evaluate.

or

<u>We</u> are going to evaluate.

[standard]   <u>We</u> students are going to evaluate the faculty.

Focus 3.2

■ Lots of truly intelligent people do not have a clue when faced with deciding whether to write *you and I* or *you and me*. The choice becomes easy, though, if you simply drop the pronoun after *and* to see how the single pronoun sounds all by itself. Your ear will then tell you which pair to use. Try it with this sentence:

(<u>You and me</u> or <u>you and I</u>?) need a vacation.

Drop the first pronoun from each pair and ask yourself, which sounds better:

<u>Me</u> need a vacation.

or

<u>I</u> need a vacation.

Clearly, "I need a vacation" is preferable. So you would choose *you and I*:

<u>You and I</u> need a vacation in Colorado.

■ Here is another example:

The Rotary Club asked (<u>Sue and I</u> or <u>Sue and me</u>?) to perform our comedy routine.

Now, **drop the first part** from both pairs and decide which sentence sounds better:

The Rotary Club asked <u>I</u> to perform our comedy routine.

or

The Rotary Club asked <u>me</u> to perform our comedy routine.

Focus 3.2 (continued)

> You would surely have no trouble in deciding on the second version. So, your choice would be *Sue and me*:
>
> The Rotary Club asked <u>Sue and me</u> to perform our comedy routine.
>
> ### A Word of Caution
>
> ■ Do not mix up the pairs and write *him and I* or *she and me*. Both pronouns in compound constructions should be in the same case—i.e., both subjective or both objective or both possessive. If you aren't sure which pronouns are in what case, see the handy list in Focus 3.1.
>
> And do not ever say *between you and I. Between you and me* is always the standard version.

How about this one?

The faculty will be evaluated by (<u>us</u> or <u>we</u>?) students.

Ask yourself:

will be evaluated by <u>we</u>?

or

will be evaluated by <u>us</u>?

Of course:

[standard]   The faculty will be evaluated by <u>us</u> students.

Here are two more:

Two seniors, Mario and (<u>I</u> or <u>me</u>?), will serve as editors.

Me will serve as editor?

or

I will serve as editor?

[standard]   Two seniors, Mario and I, will serve as editors.

The editorial board chose two seniors, Mario and (I or me?).

The board chose I?

or

The board chose me?

[standard]   The editorial board chose two seniors, Mario and me.

Using Pronouns as Predicate Nominatives

Standard usage formerly required the **subjective case** in any **complement** following the verb *to be*:

[standard]   The new editors are Mario and I.

Today, according to *Webster's Dictionary of English Usage*, "both the *It is I* and the *It's me* patterns are in reputable use and have been for a considerable time."[1] The subjective case (*I, we, he, she, they*) is used after *be* verbs in more formal situations; the objective forms (*me, us, him, her, them*) occur in speech and in more relaxed writing styles.

Using Pronouns in Comparisons

People often have trouble with pronouns in comparisons when these constructions are incomplete:

---

[1] Gilman, E. Ward, ed. *Webster's Dictionary of English Usage.* Springfield, MA: Merriam-Webster, 1989, page 568.

[nonstandard]   My sister Sally is two years older than <u>me</u>.
[standard]   My sister Sally is two years older than <u>I</u>.

If you finish the comparison in your mind before completing the sentence, you will have no trouble choosing the right pronoun. Which would you say?

Sally is older than <u>me</u> am.

or

Sally is older than <u>I</u> am.

No problem. But notice that the following sentences could both be correct, although they may have different meanings:

Pablo likes pastrami better than <u>me</u>.
Pablo likes pastrami better than <u>I</u>.

When you finish those comparisons, they come out differently:

Pablo likes pastrami better than he likes me.
Pablo likes pastrami better than I like pastrami.

So, be careful with your pronouns, or you may have someone accidentally preferring pastrami to people.

Choosing "Who" or "Whom"

Lots of people cannot decide whether to use *who* or *whom* even in fairly simple sentences. Fortunately, the substitution technique works here, also, but often you have to do some rearranging first. Consider this sentence:

(<u>Who</u> or <u>whom</u>?) did the committee select?

Like many sentences posing questions, the words in this example do not appear in the usual order, which is *subject/verb/completer*. Before using substitution, you need to turn the question into a statement having normal word order so that you can figure out whether the pronoun functions as the subject or the completer. If the pronoun turns out to be the subject, naturally you will use the subjective case, *who*; if it proves to be the completer, you will use the objective form, *whom*.

So first, to phrase the question as a statement, you say:

The committee did select (<u>who</u> or <u>whom</u>?).

Now you can see that because *committee* is the subject, the pronoun functions as the object of the verb (*did select*). Thus, the question should read:

[standard]   <u>Whom</u> did the committee select?

Sometimes sentences that are not questions also require a bit of rearranging before doing substitutions when the pronoun appears in a **dependent clause**:

Craig is a friend (<u>who</u> or <u>whom</u>?) I love dearly.

The first clause—"Craig is a friend"—needs no rearranging, but the second clause is not in the usual order. The meaning of the second clause—"(*who* or *whom*) I love dearly"—is "I love my friend dearly," because the **antecedent** of the pronoun (either *who* or *whom*) is *friend*. So, when you rearrange the clause in normal sentence order, putting the subject first and substituting *who* or *whom* for the noun *friend*, you get

I love (<u>who</u> or <u>whom</u>?) dearly.

Next, just replace the *who* or *whom* with *he* or *him*. Which would you say?

I love <u>he</u> dearly.

or

I love <u>him</u> dearly.

Him, of course. Now, if you check your list of pronoun case forms in Focus 3.1, you will find that *him* is objective; thus, you need the objective *whom*:

[standard]   Craig is a friend <u>whom</u> I love dearly.

Let's run through that procedure again with a similar example, and this time we will explain the grammar involved in rearranging the second clause:

Virginia Woolf is a novelist (<u>who</u> or <u>whom</u>?) critics admire.

The **independent clause** ("Virginia Woolf is a novelist") is in normal sentence order, but the dependent clause that makes up the rest of the sentence begins with a choice between two relative pronouns. **Relative pronouns** perform a dual function: they connect a dependent clause to an independent clause, and they also serve as **subject** or **direct object** within the dependent clause.

To find out whether the pronoun in question will be the subject or the object, you first locate the verb (by changing the time expressed in the clause, remember?). When you change the time, this dependent clause—"(who or whom) critics *admire*"—becomes "(who or whom) critics *admired*." The word changed will be the verb—in this case, *admire*.

Now, remember as well that to find the subject, you put *who* or *what* in front of the verb and ask, "*Who* or *what* admire?" The meaning of the clause tells you that *critics* admire. Thus, you have found the subject: *critics*.

Finally, ask yourself, "Critics admire *what*?" and you get (*who* or *whom*), the direct object. So, you have figured out grammatically that the pronoun in question is the object of the verb *admire*. That means you need the objective case of the pronoun—*whom*.

You will soon get the hang of rearranging clauses to get the normal sentence order, and then you can go ahead with the easy substitution method. Which would you say?

Critics admire <u>she</u>.

or

Critics admire <u>her</u>.

Her, naturally. Because *her* is the objective form, you need the objective *whom*:

[standard]   Virginia Woolf is a novelist <u>whom</u> critics admire.

An Easy Way Out. If you are writing in a hurry—taking an essay exam, for instance—and don't have time to work out the substitution technique, you can simply use *that* instead. Some people may not approve, but standard English allows this usage in all but the most formal writing today:

[standard]   Virginia Woolf is a novelist <u>that</u> critics admire.

But do not get carried away and try to use *which*. It is not acceptable to use *which* to refer to people.

Using Possessive Pronouns

Although possessive pronouns do not themselves cause any difficulty, they are often confused with the contractions of verbs having the same pronunciation but different spellings. Here are the ones most commonly confused.

Its is the possessive pronoun, and
It's is the contraction of *it is* or *it has.*

[example]   My life has lost <u>its</u> savor because <u>it's</u> boring.

Their is the possessive pronoun, and
They're is the contraction of *they are.*

[example]   <u>Their</u> feelings are hurt because <u>they're</u> losing.

Your is the possessive pronoun, and
You're is the contraction of *you are.*

[example] <u>Your</u> memory fails because <u>you're</u> not
           concentrating.

These mix-ups are easy to sort out if you will just remember
this:

NONE OF THE POSSESSIVE PERSONAL PRONOUNS USES
AN APOSTROPHE.

So, if you need to show ownership, you choose a word without
an apostrophe—a *possessive pronoun* (*its, their, your*). If you
need a pronoun-verb combination, you choose one with an
apostrophe—a *contraction* (*it's, they're, you're*).

3.B   MAKING PRONOUN REFERENCE CLEAR

Because pronouns depend on the nouns they rename to
supply their meaning, writers must be sure that the **reference**
is always clear. Problems often occur when there are two nouns
in a sentence and the pronoun could refer to either one:

[unclear] The teacher told the student to be sure to put
           <u>her</u> name on the paper.

This sentence can mean two things:

> The teacher told the student, "Be sure to put <u>your</u>
> name on the paper."
> The teacher told the student, "Be sure to put <u>my</u> name
> on the paper."

Sometimes pronoun reference can be unclear because the
pronoun gets too far away from its noun:

[unclear] I discovered our gray striped cat on the
           counter eating pizza that I'm crazy about.
[clear]   I discovered our gray striped cat that I'm
           crazy about on the counter eating pizza.

And sometimes a writer will forget entirely to put in the antecedent:

[vague] I quit school because <u>they</u> went out of <u>their</u> way
         to pick on me.

                              antecedent
[clear] I quit school because the principal and the

         antecedent
         math teacher went out of <u>their</u> way to pick on me.

Be sure that the **antecedent** (the noun that a pronoun refers to) is present—preferably in the same sentence.

Using "This" and "Which"

The pronouns *this* and *which* are exceedingly handy for referring to something previously mentioned—so handy, in fact, that writers sometimes neglect to specify precisely what *this* or *which* means.

Focus 3.3

USAGE NOTE: WHAT DOES "THIS" MEAN?

- *This* is a pronoun and should have a clear antecedent—that is, a word or word group that it replaces in the sentence. Here is an example:

  I will provide you with a magic laser gun. This will protect you from creatures of Phoros, Pecunias, and Gordo.

  Obviously, the antecedent of *this* is *magic laser gun*. (Strictly speaking, the antecedent is *gun*, and the adjectives are extra.)
     Sometimes, the antecedent for the word *this* is more elaborate but still quite clear. For example, you might write

  Fire the magic laser gun while rolling the stone from the entrance of the dragon's cave and chanting the spell. This will repel Lumbargites.

Focus 3.3 (continued)

This refers to the whole process of firing the gun, rolling the stone, and chanting the spell. Few people would disagree. If, however, you meant only that *chanting the spell* would repel Lumbargites, you have misled your readers with your use of the word *this*.

Specify "This" What

■ In any situation where the meaning of *this* could be mistaken, as in the preceding example, you are safer writing a noun after the *this*. Some examples will show how the noun clarifies meaning:

Fire the magic laser gun while rolling the stone from the entrance of the dragon's cave and chanting the spell. This <u>chanting</u> will repel Lumbargites.
Fire the magic laser gun while rolling the stone from the entrance of the dragon's cave and chanting the spell. This <u>process</u> will repel Lumbargites.

■ A general rule is that pronouns must refer unmistakably to their antecedents. Any looseness in your *this* reference can produce confusion or unintentional humor:

My Uncle Steve was buried at the age of twenty-seven along with the twisted steering wheel of his beloved racing car. I never thought I would live to see this.

This could refer to the simple fact of Uncle Steve's death, his youth at the time of his death, the meaningless cause of his demise, the ludicrous conditions of his burial, or the waste of a salvageable steering wheel.

[vague]   *The Handmaid's Tale* presents a futuristic society
          where the only acceptable roles for females in-
          volve pleasing men, doing housework, and
          producing babies. This makes the novel chilling
          reading.
[clear]   *The Handmaid's Tale* presents a futuristic society
          where the only acceptable roles for females in-
          volve pleasing men, doing housework, and
          producing babies. This oppression of women
          makes the novel chilling reading.

Try to get in the habit of always writing a noun after *this.* In
other words, always specify this *what*: *this problem, this case,
this benefit, this principle, this need,* and so on.

  The imprecise use of *which* is similar:

[vague]   Sandy whispered all through the movie, went out
          for popcorn three times, and propped her feet on
          the seat in front of her, which especially annoyed
          Daryl.
[clear]   Sandy, who whispered all through the movie and
          went out for popcorn three times, annoyed Daryl
          especially by propping her feet on the back of his
          seat.

During the revising process, you should check every *this* and
which to be sure the meaning you intend is precisely clear.

3.C   ACHIEVING AGREEMENT

  Just as verbs are supposed to agree with their subjects, pronouns are supposed to agree with their **antecedents** (the nouns
that they refer to or identify). Thus, a singular antecedent
would be followed by a singular pronoun; a plural antecedent
would be followed by a plural pronoun:

[singular]   George is figuring his income tax.
[plural]   Americans must pay their income taxes by
             April 15.

When two singular antecedents are connected by *or* or *nor*, the pronoun referring to them is still singular; when the antecedents are connected by *and*, the pronoun will be plural:

[singular]   Neither Sid <u>nor</u> Sam is going to pay <u>his</u> taxes.
[plural]   Sid <u>and</u> Sam think <u>they</u> can outsmart the IRS.

Using Indefinite Pronouns

A couple of the **indefinite pronouns** (*all, many*) cause no trouble, because they can be either singular or plural, depending on your meaning:

[singluar]   All of <u>my</u> strength is drained.
[plural]   All of <u>their</u> savings have been wiped out.

Collective nouns (such as *committee, family, group, team*) are equally agreeable because, again, the writer gets to decide whether the pronoun should be singular or plural according to meaning:

[singular]   The team worked hard to get <u>its</u> spirits up
             before the big game.
[plural]   The team quarreled about <u>their</u> many mistakes.

But the following indefinite pronouns have been decreed grammatically singular—although often they are clearly plural in meaning:

everyone	anyone	everybody	none
anybody	no one	neither	either

According to traditional grammar, the following sentences are correct, but according to logic, they have serious failings:

After my talk, <u>everyone</u> applauded, and I was glad <u>he</u> did.
As soon as <u>everybody</u> finished <u>his</u> test, the instructor passed among <u>him</u> and collected it.
<u>Everybody</u> liked the steak, but <u>he</u> did not eat the prune whip.

This illogical rule finally became so difficult for grammarians to enforce that people in high places began to ignore it with increasing frequency. As *Webster's Dictionary of English Usage* points out, "the plural *they, their, them* with an indefinite pronoun as referent is in common standard use."[2] So you may now correctly write

[standard]   Everyone must buckle their seatbelts by law in
              Texas.
[standard]   Neither of my parents will admit their obvious
              faults.
[standard]   None of my friends will even visit their families.

Using Gender-Free Pronouns

Standard written English still requires a singular pronoun to agree with an indefinite pronoun when the meaning is singular. And standard English used to require that writers use the masculine singular pronouns (*he, him, his*) to refer to any singular antecedent, regardless of whether it included women:

[exclusive]   Each student must hold his own ticket.
[exclusive]   No one will be allowed to take the exam
              early unless he has an official excuse.

Because such usages, which make women linguistically invisible, are sexist, many writers have gone back to the older practice of using both pronouns to refer to singular antecedents that include both men and women:

[inclusive]   Each student must hold his or her own ticket.
[inclusive]   No one will be allowed to take the exam early
              unless he or she has an official excuse.

[2] Gilman, E. Ward, ed. *Webster's Dictionary of English Usage.* Springfield, MA: Merriam-Webster, 1989, page 52.

Because this construction is a bit wordy, you would not want to use it often. You can avoid it most of the time by writing in the plural:

[singular]   <u>Every</u> American may openly express <u>his</u> or <u>her</u> own opinion—even to criticize the government.

[plural]   <u>All</u> Americans may openly express <u>their</u> own opinions—even to criticize the government.

[plural]   As Americans <u>we</u> may openly express <u>our</u> own opinions—even to criticize the government.

Many times writers stick in a sexist pronoun that can simply be eliminated:

[sexist]   <u>No one</u> will be allowed to take <u>his</u> exam early.

[nonsexist]   <u>No one</u> will be allowed to take the exam early.

The easiest thing to do, though, is to write in the plural, and the whole problem disappears:

[nonsexist]   No <u>students</u> will be allowed to take <u>their</u> <u>exams</u> early.

Possessive Pronouns with Gerunds

If you want to write with perfect accuracy, you will use the possessive case before a **gerund** (a word ending in -*ing* that sounds like a verb but functions as a noun):

Melvin was insistent about <u>my calling</u> right away.

Many people would write that sentence this way:

Melvin was insistent about <u>me calling</u> right away.

Although standard English allows this usage now in informal writing, a number of people still prefer the possessive before gerunds:

> Their refusing to compromise caused the negotiations to fail.
> I thought his leaving early was extremely rude.

Nouns also should be made possessive before gerunds:

> Danny's hammering in the basement confused the dog.
> We chortled at the dog's racing to the front door to see who was there.

Chapter 4
Modifiers

A **modifier** is a word, phrase, or clause that limits or qualifies the meaning of another word or word group. All of the essential parts of a sentence—the **subject**, the **verb**, and the **completers**—can be expanded by adding modifiers, which describe, intensify, define, change, restrict, identify, and expand the meaning of any element in the sentence. As you can see, modifiers are important and complex. A writer also has a lot of leeway in selecting and arranging them. You will become a better writer by learning to choose appropriate modifiers and using them with clarity and precision.

4.A KEEPING ADJECTIVES AND ADVERBS STRAIGHT

Sometimes you make yourself sound uneducated by using an **adjective** when you should use an **adverb**. Here are some examples:

Sandy walked down the sleazy waterfront quick.

This stupid Christmas song makes me feel awful sad.

Mark makes real delightful phone calls.

Quick, *awful*, and *real* are in the inappropriate form. The sentences are in informal English, which is fine for many purposes, but their written form should be this:

Sandy walked down the sleazy waterfront quickly.

This stupid Christmas song makes me feel awfully
sad.
Mark makes really delightful phone calls.

The written forms should include *-ly* endings because of the
words they modify. To *modify* means to alter, qualify, limit,
or describe.

How Adjectives Function

An adjective, in standard English, only modifies a noun
or nounlike word. In the preceding sample sentences, some
adjectives are *sleazy*, *stupid*, *Christmas* (because it modifies
song), *sad*, and *delightful*. An adjective usually appears before
the word it modifies:

The <u>dangerous</u> atmosphere excites Jane.

It can also appear after a **linking verb** and modify the subject
of the sentence; then it is called a **predicate adjective**:

Laura's mother looks <u>frisky</u>.

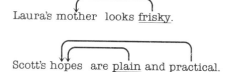

Scott's hopes are <u>plain</u> and <u>practical</u>.

How Adverbs Function

An adverb, in standard English, modifies almost anything
except a noun:

Susan <u>regretfully</u> resigned from her job.
Her <u>spitefully</u> resentful boss <u>finally</u> made <u>too</u> many
demands, <u>too</u> <u>thoughtlessly</u>.

In the preceding examples, an adverb modifies a verb
(*resigned*), an adjective (*resentful*), another verb (*made*),
another adjective (*many*), and another adverb (*thoughtlessly*).

Adverbs modify by giving information about time (when), place (where), manner (how), frequency (how often), and cause (why).

Words that modify adjectives and adverbs are also called **qualifiers** or **intensifiers**. With the exception of a few words, such as *really*, qualifiers are rarely used to modify verbs. Instead, they qualify or intensify the meaning of adjectives and adverbs:

Jay walked <u>very</u> slowly.

That test was <u>too</u> difficult.

Sula is <u>quite</u> capable of doing the work.

Other common qualifiers are *rather, fairly, mighty, somewhat, still, even, some, much,* and *no*.

Adverb Forms

Adverbs frequently end in *-ly, -ward,* and *-wise*:

hopefully	backward
sideways	clockwise

The *-ly* endings are the ones many people often leave off accidentally, causing the words to seem like ill-used adjectives. Sometimes the adverb form is completely different from the adjective: *well* is the adverb form of *good*:

Laura's mother dresses oddly but well.

And some *-ly* adverbs are used as qualifiers to modify adjectives:

especially easy
absolutely necessary
politically expedient
particularly helpful

Knowing When To Use an Adverb

How do you know when you should use an adverb? The best way, when in doubt, is to use the process of elimination. If an adjective is what you want, there should be a noun in the neighborhood. Nouns can be made singular and plural, and

Focus 4.1

USAGE NOTE: DO I USE "WELL" OR "GOOD"?

■ Sometimes it's not obvious whether to use an **adjective**, like *good*, or its related **adverb** (*well*). If the word describes the manner of the action denoted by the verb, then you use an adverb in formal writing:

This student writes <u>well</u>. [not <u>good</u>]

Yolanda hurt her neck <u>badly</u>. [not <u>bad</u>]

Pat's dog was barking <u>loudly</u>. [not <u>loud</u>]

But if the word is a **subjective complement**, which comes after a linking verb and modifies the subject of the sentence, then it's an adjective:

This peanut butter pizza tastes <u>good</u>.

Tony feels <u>bad</u> about his missing parakeet.

The adverb *badly* is often used with the linking verb *feel* in speech and informal writing, but in formal writing you should use *feel bad*.

Focus 4.1 (continued)

- In the sentence

  I don't feel well.

  the word *well* is an adjective meaning "in good health."
  But in the sentence

  Reggie doesn't sing well.

  it is an adverb meaning "skillfully" or "proficiently."
- If the **modifier** in question is used to intensify the meaning
  of a verb, adjective, or adverb, you use an *-ly* form in
  formal writing:

[informal]   I <u>sure</u> like your new hairdo.

[formal]   I <u>certainly</u> like your new hairdo.

[informal]   That was a <u>real</u> good movie.

[formal]   That was a <u>really</u> good movie.

they sound all right with such words as *the*, *a*, *this*, and *that*
before them. Look at this list of examples showing accurate
adjective and adverb use:

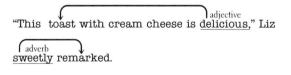

"This toast with cream cheese is <u>delicious</u>," Liz   adjective

<u>sweetly</u> remarked.   adverb

Sondra <u>slowly</u> licked her lips <u>suggestively</u>, looking
at Sam.   adverb   adverb

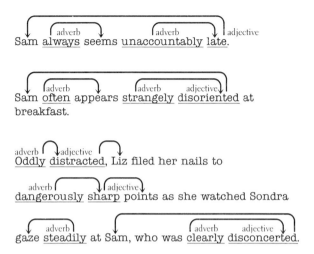

In those examples, Sam is described by the words *late, disoriented,* and *disconcerted* (all adjectives). The toast is *delicious,* Liz is *distracted,* and her nail points are *sharp* (all adjectives); but adverbs are needed to modify Sondra's licking and gazing (verbs) and to describe the exact nature of Liz's distraction and Sam's disorientation and disconcertedness, because those conditions are expressed by adjectives, not by nouns. And *dangerously* intensifies the meaning of the adjective *sharp,* just as *clearly* qualifies *disconcerted.*

No one can deny the rough charm of such spoken statements as, "You dress nice enough for any mortal man, and I sure admire you," and "You did real good on the ACT test." However, when putting such sentiments into writing, using the adverbial forms is a good idea:

> You dress nicely enough for any mortal man, and I surely admire you.
>
> You did really well on the ACT test.

Well said.

4.B   AVOIDING DOUBLE NEGATIVES

Although other languages use multiple negatives as a matter of course and spoken English uses them to indicate emphasis ("I don't want that good-for-nothing fool near me nohow!"), in written English most double negatives are considered **nonstandard**. At one time the preference for single negatives was rationalized using mathematical logic: two negatives, like two negative numbers, were said to cancel each other out and make a positive statement. Examples such as the following were said to be logically confusing:

> I won't give you no more expensive perfume, Gladys; it just draws mosquitoes.

> Gladys can't scarcely help but blame the tropical weather for her setbacks.

Actually, confusion is not the problem, because no native speaker of English would misunderstand those sentences. Tradition is the problem, and though we encourage you to express nontraditional ideas if you are so inclined, we advise you to follow grammatical tradition if you do not want to detract from your message. In addition to such obvious words as *not* and *never*, negatives also include the adverbs *barely*, *scarcely*, and *hardly* and the preposition *but* (meaning "except").

In lively and forceful speech among intimate company, you might exclaim, "I'm not no fool!" However, that sentence is not acceptable even in informal writing: it contains a double negative. The prohibition against this kind of double negative in writing is extremely strong, and you should make sure that your sentences do not contain them.

Standard written English does permit double negation when the two negatives combine to make a positive understatement. When *not* modifies an adjective or adverb with a negative prefix (such as *un-* or *in-*), it neutralizes the negative force of the modifier:

> Her resignation was <u>not unexpected</u>.

> He did <u>not</u> speak <u>indecisively</u>.

A few other negative combinations are also acceptable in standard English:

> We cannot afford not to speak out.

4.C   USING COMPARATIVE AND SUPERLATIVE MODIFIERS

Adjectives and adverbs come in three forms: we use the **positive form** to simply state that someone is a *happy* camper; we use the **comparative form** to say that one camper is *happier* than another; we use the **superlative form** to say that one camper is the *happiest* of them all.

To make the comparative and superlative forms, you add *-er* and *-est* to one-syllable modifiers (*younger, youngest*) or use a premodifier with words of three syllables or more (*more beautiful, most beautiful*). Many two-syllable words can take either form (*politer, politest; more polite, most polite*).

Double Comparisons

You do not want to be redundant by using both *more* and the *-er* ending or *most* and the *-est* ending:

[redundant]	My answer is <u>more better</u> than yours.
[standard]	My answer is <u>better</u> than yours.

[redundant]	He is the <u>most daffiest</u> person I know.
[standard]	He is the <u>daffiest</u> person I know.

In formal writing, use the comparative for two items only (*the younger of the two brothers*) and the superlative for more than two (*the youngest of the five brothers*).

Some common modifiers have irregular comparative and superlative forms:

Positive	Comparative	Superlative
good	better	best
well	better	best
bad	worse	worst
far	farther (further)	farthest (furthest)
little	less	least
much	more	most

Modifiers That Do Not Compare

Some writers insist that certain adjectives and adverbs cannot be compared. These people maintain that something is either *unique* (or *complete* or *perfect*) or it is not, and there are no degrees in between. Yet even in formal writing we find such expressions as *a more perfect union* or *the most extreme poverty*. If you want to be safe, it is better not to use the comparative or superlative of such words as these in formal writing.

4.D   ARRANGING MODIFIERS EFFECTIVELY

A **modifier** qualifies, limits, or describes another word or group of words, and it should be placed as closely as possible to whatever it modifies. Most importantly, whatever it modifies has to *be there* in the sentence you write.

Dangling Modifiers

In the following examples, the modifiers are whole phrases at the beginnings of sentences and should modify the first noun (which is the subject):

[dangling]   Born in 1923, *The Naked and the Dead* was Norman Mailer's first novel, published in 1948.

The novel was not born in 1923; Norman Mailer was. But a reader could easily think that perhaps *The Naked and the Dead* was first started in 1923 and took twenty-five years to complete or get published. To be clear, you should place the modifier close to the words it modifies:

[clear] Born in 1923, Norman Mailer published his first novel, *The Naked and the Dead*, in 1948, when he was only twenty-five.

Focus 4.2

WRITING TIP: WHERE IS THE BEST PLACE TO PUT A MODIFIER?

■ You can ensure the correct interpretation of your sentences by paying close attention to where you place your **modifiers** (words, phrases, and clauses that alter or clarify the sense of another word or word group). Consider how the meaning changes in these two sentences when the modifying phrase is shifted to a different position:

Several times the teacher told him to proofread his paper.
The teacher told him to proofread his paper several times.

■ Even if there is no serious danger of misinterpretation, a carelessly placed modifier can make a sentence more difficult to understand:

[puzzling] He said that he loved her in a calm way.
[clearer]   He said in a calm way that he loved her.

Putting the adverbial phrase *in a calm way* next to the verb *said* illustrates the general rule about where to place a modifier: **as close as possible to the word it modifies**.

Focus 4.2 (continued)

If you do not abide by this principle, you may wind up with some unintentionally humorous results, such as this headline:

```
Sisters Reunited After 18 Years in Checkout Line
at Supermarket
```

or this announcement from a church bulletin:

```
The church will hold a memorial service
next Wednesday evening at 7 p.m. for Martha
Hawkins, who died last week, at the request of
her family.
```

■ Sometimes a sentence has more than one interpretation if a modifier is positioned between two words so that it could be construed to modify either one:

```
Our professor told us Friday he might give a
quiz.
```

Moving the modifier will clear up the ambiguity:

```
Friday our professor told us he might give a
quiz.
Our professor told us he might give a quiz
Friday.
```

Readers automatically assume that the first noun after an introductory modifier is the one that the modifier goes with:

[dangling]   After a lot of hard studying, the test was still
             too difficult.

The hard studying is not attributed to anyone. The relative positions of the modifier and the noun seem to imply that the test did the studying. It does not solve the problem to put the person who did the studying at the end of the sentence:

[dangling]   **After a lot of hard studying, the test was still too difficult for Tiffany.**

The modifier, "After a lot of hard studying," is too far from the word it modifies, "Tiffany." The sentence should read:

[clear]   **After a lot of hard studying, Tiffany still found the test too difficult.**

Misplaced Modifiers

In the next two examples, the modified noun appears in the sentence, but in the wrong place. The noun should be as close as possible to the modifier, so that no misunderstanding can occur.

[misplaced]   **Having a clever and adorable tutor, the final exam was a breeze for Tiffany.**

The exam didn't have a tutor; Tiffany did. So the sentence should read:

[clear]   **Having a clever and adorable tutor, Tiffany breezed through the final exam.**

[also clear]   **With the help of a clever and adorable tutor, Tiffany breezed through the final exam.**

Either revision is fine. Here is another misplaced modifier:

[misplaced]   **To maintain a C average, the tutor had to meet with Tiffany three times a week.**

It was Tiffany, not the tutor, who needed the C average, so the sentence should say:

[clear]   To maintain a C average, Tiffany had to meet with her tutor three times a week.

Sometimes the modifier can be misplaced or dangle in the middle or at the end of a sentence:

[misplaced]   I saw a number of lively altercations <u>strolling down the streets of Paris.</u>

[clear]   Strolling down the streets of Paris, I saw a number of lively altercations.

[misplaced]   Several important people <u>at the age of eight</u> disappeared from my life.

[clear]   When I was eight years old, several important people disappeared from my life.

Chapter 5
Punctuation

Unlike speakers, writers cannot rely on **intonation**, gesture, or facial expression to help them present their ideas. The only aid that a writer has—besides word choice and word order—is punctuation. The conventions of punctuating written sentences are not numerous, but they are complicated and flexible enough to give some writers more trouble than help. The most used—and misused—marks of punctuation are the comma, the apostrophe, and quotation marks. Writers must understand the fundamentals of using these marks if they want to write clear, readable prose.

5.A DECIDING ABOUT COMMAS BETWEEN MAIN SENTENCE ELEMENTS

Many people have been victims of the misleading advice that commas belong wherever you would pause when you read a sentence aloud. This rule can lead to certain ruin, as far as punctuation goes. In two major places, a comma may sound natural, but these locations alone do not justify adding the comma. These places are between the **subject** and the **verb** and between the verb and its **completer**. Subject/verb/completer comprise the three main sentence parts, as shown in the following examples:

```
Steve's cat  /  makes  /  a horrible noise.
The cat  /  gives  /  Bumper the creeps.
```

The cat / is / obnoxious.
The cat / is / a rude beast.
The cat / yowls. (This sentence has only two of the three parts, because the verb does not need a completer.)

Finding Sentence Elements

Even without knowing elaborate terminology, you can divide sentences into their main parts. In the following examples, draw one line where these sentences seem to split naturally.

A man of your age should have a little money in the bank.

Running off to the Virgin Islands every Christmas will not solve your problems.

Life-style advice from a certified public accountant may not be completely reliable.

The first split you are likely to identify is probably between the subject and the predicate:

A man of your age / should have a little money in the bank.

Running off to the Virgin Islands every Christmas / will not solve your problems.

Life-style advice from a certified public accountant / may not be completely reliable.

If you were asked to make another split, it would probably be between the verb and the completer:

A man of your age / should have / a little money in the bank.

Running off to the Virgin Islands every Christmas / will not solve / your problems.

Life-style advice from a certified public accountant / may not be / completely reliable.

Commas in Long Sentences

In long sentences, these three major parts may seem to need commas between them, but they do not. You may feel tempted to write something like this:

> The problem with dating only men who have recently done long terms in prison for armed robbery and similar crimes, is not just that they forget to pay for their food in restaurants.

> Men who have been consistently institutionalized from an early age frequently feel, that they have lost the capacity to express tender emotions.

Actually, neither of those sentences needs a comma. Sometimes an **interrupter** or long sentence opener necessitates a comma or two:

```
                ─────long sentence opener─────────
After seven years in the penitentiary, Dave had a
problem with his self-concept.
```

```
                ───────────────interrupter──────────────────
Dave, who gets nicked for every crime he commits,
will never stop picking fights with large
strangers in sleazy bars.
```

If you suspect that you may be strewing unnecessary commas throughout your prose, here are some ways to check. If you see a comma *directly* before the main verb of a sentence, trace back and make sure that comma has a partner earlier on, because legitimate commas in that position come in pairs, as in the preceding example. A lone comma is adequate when the subject and verb appear *after* that comma, as in the sentence beginning with "After seven years in the penitentiary."

Finally, remember Mark Twain's advice about the comma: "When in doubt, leave it out."

Commas in Compound Sentences

Sometimes sentences themselves (independent clauses) are elements within a sentence; these constructions are called **compound sentences**. Here are some examples:

> Angela and Scott set up housekeeping together to save money, and rumors about their relationship started flying.

> Their fellow graduate students suspected a romance between them, but no such relationship really exists.

In compound sentences the independent clauses are connected with a **coordinating conjunction** (*and, or, but, nor, for, yet, so*). You should place a comma before the coordinating conjunction in compound sentences.

5.B   SETTING OFF SENTENCE ELEMENTS WITH PUNCTUATION

Commas are most frequently used to set off elements (or structures) in sentences. Learn to look at a basic English **sentence**—with a **subject**, **verb**, and **completer**—as a single structure:

> Liz loves cleaning the house.

To that structure can be added others in the beginning, middle, and ending positions:

[beginning]	Though it seems odd to most of us, Liz loves cleaning the house.
[middle]	Liz, who hates to do laundry, loves cleaning the house.
[ending]	Liz loves cleaning the house, a preference we find hard to believe.

These additional structures are set off from the main sentence by commas. If you leave the commas out, the reader may be confused or disconcerted, because your punctuation is not marking off where the main clause begins and ends.

Focus 5.1

WRITING TIP: WHERE DO I PUT THE COMMAS?

- If you toss in commas whenever you feel the need, you are probably using too many—or perhaps too few. Commas, like all marks of punctuation, guide your readers through your prose. Whenever you use a comma in an unusual way, you run the risk of misleading your readers who expect standard punctuation.
- So the thing to do is learn the standard uses for commas in English sentences. The system, which is surprisingly simple, boils down to this:

Use a Comma

- After an introductory word or phrase, a dependent clause, or a long phrase at the beginning.

  Well, I have changed my mind about the movie.
  Dr. Malarkey, your argument greatly influenced me.
  In the first place, you helped me see the true meaning.
  Before you go to the movie, you should read the book.
  After seeing that confusing but fascinating movie, I think I need to read the book.

- Before a word, phrase, or clause tacked on at the end.

  I was hopelessly confused, nevertheless.
  I could not understand the film at all, not one tiny bit.
  Can you explain the ending, Dr. Malarkey?

Focus 5.1 (continued)

Movies are better on a big screen, don't you think?
I value your opinion, whatever it may be.

- Before and after a dependent clause, phrase, or word that interrupts.

    Lori, who is a film buff, explained the movie to me.
    Lori, as far as I can tell, knows a lot about movies.
    Lori, however, knows nothing about books.

- Before a coordinating conjunction (*and, but, or, for, nor, yet, so*) followed by an independent clause.

    I like most American movies, but I often find foreign films endlessly confusing.

- Between words, phrases, or short, balanced clauses in series.

    Al crunches popcorn, candy, and corn chips during movies.
    Then he slurps a cola, burps loudly, and falls asleep.
    I yell at him, I plead with him, I reason with him, but he refuses to change his behavior.

- To separate a direct quotation from your introduction of it.

    Dwayne says, "Love me, love my dog," and he means it.

- Only rarely you may need a comma for clarity.

    The thing to ask yourself is, is this trip necessary?

(continued)

Focus 5.1 (continued)

Do NOT Use a Comma

- Between *subject and verb* or *verb and complement*.

[misleading]   A lively lecture followed by a good question-and-answer session, is entertaining and instructive.

[misleading]   I was told by several trustworthy people, that this speaker would not be boring.

- Around a restrictive dependent clause (one necessary to the meaning of the sentence).

[restrictive]   People who compose on word processors can use spell checkers to catch their mispellings.

[nonrestrictive]   Sid, who composes on a word processor, is too lazy to use the spell checker.

- Before *and* when it connects compound subjects or objects.

[misleading]   His laziness about spelling, and his inability to proofread make Sid's writing sound illiterate.

[misleading]   I asked my roommate to help me proofread, and thus improved my writing considerably.

- As a general rule, follow Mark Twain's advice: "When in doubt, leave it out."

Compare the following examples with sentences in your own writing to see whether you are using commas in similar places.

Commas Setting Off Beginning Structures

Liz, I think your skirt is too tight.

Finally, some comments should go unspoken.

In general, total honesty is not always appropriate.

When a person's feelings are likely to be hurt, you should consider whether being completely honest is really imperative.

Before blurting out your opinion of another person's appearance, look at yourself.

Commas Setting Off Mid-Sentence Interrupters

Your insulting remark, Liz, will come back to haunt you.

Honesty, we think, should always be tempered by kindness.

Mr. O'Malley, my friend from school, has taught me a lot about etiquette.

Telling the truth is sometimes, truthfully, an excuse for being cruel.

A noncommittal remark, in the end, may be the proper response to questions about personal appearance.

George, taking into account my frame of mind, told me that my swimsuit had beautiful colors.

My swimsuit, which is bright red and flaming orange, does fit a bit tightly.

In the preceding examples the commas work in pairs. Be careful that you do not mark one end of the interrupter and not the other.

In those last two sentences, the interrupters (the parts between commas) could be dropped out of the sentence without changing the overall meaning, like this:

George told me that my swimsuit had beautiful colors.

My swimsuit does fit a bit tightly.

You can use this dropout rule to decide whether to enclose an interrupter in commas.

Commas Setting Off Ending Structures

> We ridiculed Mr. O'Malley, thinking he was a fuddy-duddy.
>
> George's standards of beauty are extremely traditional, which makes him the pickiest of us all.

In these sentences, the commas set off the endings to avoid possible confusion. The ending structures, like interrupters, are comments that add to the main sentence without changing its basic meaning.

Using Dashes and Parentheses

Sometimes you may experiment with using dashes or parentheses instead of commas to set off structures. Dashes will emphasize the information within them; parentheses will de-emphasize the material:

> We had one more task to do—an incredibly difficult one.
>
> Asking Herbert to leave—although an absolute necessity—proved close to impossible.
>
> Asking Herbert (our houseguest) to leave required plenty of tact and sensitivity—as well as firmness.

Focus 5.2

USAGE NOTE: WHAT IS THE DIFFERENCE BETWEEN A COLON AND A SEMICOLON?

■ Actually, there is so much difference that you might more accurately ask, "What is the *same* about a colon and a semicolon?" Perhaps the most prevailing commonality between these punctuation marks is that both confuse the everyday writer to the point of distraction.

Semicolon Sense

■ The *semicolon* marks the separation between two independent sentences whose relationship in meaning is close.

Focus 5.2 (continued)

Independent is the important word here. A semicolon is used only between two complete sentences.

Stanley, you must rethink your strategy; you are losing more games than you are winning.

Amelia felt herself fainting into the strong arms of her enemy; to keep herself alert, she thought of punctuation rules.

The hero seems sure of himself; the heroine knows he is not.

Without semicolons, these examples would need to be rephrased to make clear the relationships in meaning:

Stanley, you must rethink your strategy because you are losing more games than you are winning.

Amelia felt herself fainting into the strong arms of her enemy and began thinking of punctuation rules to keep herself alert.

The hero seems sure of himself, but the heroine knows he is not.

In nineteenth-century writing, you will see many examples of what people now condemn as a *semicolon fragment*:

Sandpipers chased the surf down the beach and ran from it as it rose; playfully daring it to wet their tiny black feet, harmlessly provoking it to do so.

Because the second part is not a complete sentence, the semicolon is inappropriate by modern standards. Today, a comma or dash would take its place.

(continued)

Focus 5.2 (continued)

Colon Cues

■ Like the semicolon, the **colon** implies a close relationship
in meaning between two sentence parts. However, the
parts need not both be independent clauses, and the relationship
is more explicit: it must be a relationship of equality. Think
of the colon as punctuation's equivalent of the equal sign
in mathematics.

Our ideal candidate has five qualities: honesty,
warm-heartedness, intelligence, diplomacy, and
taste.

The tension was unbearable: two of my ex-
girlfriends, one with her new husband, appeared
in the courtroom unexpectedly.

A married couple should have no secrets: they
should tell each other everything.

As the first example shows, a colon before a list appears
after a complete sentence introducing the list. It does not
belong before a list when the introduction to the list is not
independent:

[no colon]   Our ideal candidate has qualities such as
             honesty, warm-heartedness, intelligence,
             diplomacy, and taste.

[no colon]   Richard asked me to bring the guacamole,
             the onion dip, and the sour cream.

5.C   USING APOSTROPHES

Apostrophes cause more problems than any other mark of
punctuation, and some intelligent and sophisticated individuals still feel shaky about using them. If you take a step-by-step
look at apostrophe use, most of your confusion can be straight-
ened out.

Possessives

As you have no doubt heard before, apostrophes are used with **nouns** to show possession. Actually, it would be more appropriate to say that the *'s* ending is a substitute for an *of the* or *of* phrase. Here are some examples:

the dimensions of the room   the room's dimensions
the best movie of the year   the year's best movie
the offer of the sleazy   the sleazy bartender's
  bartender   offer

Plural Possessives

In the preceding examples, you probably experienced no difficulty understanding the addition of the *'s* ending. Problems begin, though, because of all the other uses of the letter *s*. This letter also frequently signifies a noun's *plural* form. As a general rule, **do not use an apostrophe when you form a plural noun**: *three bartenders, two dictionaries, two complaining roommates.*

Now, what if the bartenders, dictionaries, and roommates need to be in possessive form? Then an apostrophe is needed:

three bartenders' tips
two dictionaries' conflicting definitions of *romance*
two complaining roommates' difficulties

In these cases, you do not need to add another *s* after the apostrophe, simply because you would not pronounce it aloud.

Usage varies, however, for *singular* nouns that end in *s*. On the whole, you are probably safer to follow the general practice for making singular nouns possessive and add the apostrophe and an *s*:

the boss's son   Burns's poetry
Iris's videotapes   Dickens's novels

The traditional exceptions, which take just the apostrophe, are

Jesus' teachings	Socrates' death
for goodness' sake	Moses' commandments
for conscience' sake	Xerxes' defeat

When you need to write a word that is both plural and possessive, deciding where to put the apostrophe can be difficult. The problem is solved if you follow a strict order of operations, like solving a problem in algebra. The trick is to *first* write down the plural form; *then* add either 's or an apostrophe alone. **Never move backwards to put in an apostrophe once you have written the plural form**.

Singular noun	Plural noun	Plural possessive
lady	ladies	ladies' gloves
child	children	children's antics
man	men	men's weaknesses
family	families	families' problems

Possessives Without Apostrophes

Not all possessives require apostrophes. **Personal pronouns** that show possession are apostrophe-free, including *his*, *hers*, *theirs*, *ours*, *yours*, and *its*. *Its* is a possessive pronoun that you should always check for correctness:

Commercialism has drained Christmas of its true meaning.
Bob's T-shirt is notable for its bad taste.

Telling Plurals from Possessives

How can you tell whether a word is possessive or plural? A **possessive** acts like an adjective, whereas a plural is a noun (nominal). That is, the possessive form of a noun will nearly always have another noun after it. Thus, the following reasoning is used in punctuating the phrase *two months' vacation*:

1. Because there is a noun after the word *months,* it should be possessive.
2. Now, because there is more than one month involved (two), you have a word that is both plural and possessive.
3. So you write the complete plural, *months.*
4. Then you add an apostrophe: *two months' vacation.*
5. You add no *s* after the apostrophe because you would not speak a second *s* sound out loud.

As you write and edit, if you will think through each case using this step-by-step method, the correct use of apostrophes in possessives will soon come naturally.

Contractions

The other use of the apostrophe involves *contractions,* which are combinations of verbs or auxiliaries plus other words, such as *can't* (can + not), *isn't* (is + not), *Harry's* (Harry + is), *he'll* (he + will). The apostrophe goes in where the letter or letters came out in making the combination, not where the space would have been:

    didn't (not did'nt)
    won't (not wo'nt)
    hasn't (not has'nt)
    wouldn't (not would'nt)

Most people consider contractions as *informal usage.* However, almost all writing contains some of them, as this book does. Years ago, you would not have found a grammar book that used contractions, but their acceptability has broadened. If your writing is sprinkled with them, though, you should make sure that a very informal style is appropriate for your purpose and audience. Much academic writing is fairly formal and includes few or no contractions.

Maverick Apostrophes

We must mention one maverick use of the apostrophe, which unfortunately muddies the waters. Many people use an apostrophe to make the plurals of numerals, letters, words used as words, and abbreviations, even though this usage contradicts the usual rules for plurals:

Your 5's look like 8's to me.
This sentence has four *and*'s in it.
His last name contains three *m*'s.
The 1960's were an exciting time to be alive.
He claims that he holds three Ph.D.'s.

This idiosyncratic use of the apostrophe is considered standard, although adding only an *s* is also correct and is much more grammatically consistent:

It is not clear who your *shes* refer to in this sentence.
I love '50s rock and roll.
Melita received all As on her report card.

5.D   USING QUOTATION MARKS

If you want to report the actual words that somebody has spoken or written, you need to use quotation marks. It is customary to accompany quoted material with a *reporting tag*, such as "she said" or "he replied." These reporting tags can appear in one of three positions, and the rules for punctuating quoted discourse relate to the placement of the reporting tag.

Reporting Tag at the Beginning

You usually put a comma after the reporting tag and before the initial quotation marks:

Samuel Johnson observed, "Marriage has many pains, but celibacy has no pleasures."

If the quotation ends the sentence, you put a period, a question mark, an exclamation mark, or a dash before the final quotation marks:

> The speaker warned us, "Tomorrow will be too late."
> The teacher asked, "Have you finished your tests?"
> The crowd cheered, "Long live Pee Wee Herman!"
> Liza said, "I have done my share, but you—"

The dash in this last example indicates that the speaker stopped in mid-sentence.

If a question mark or exclamation mark belongs to the whole sentence, not to the quoted material, put the end punctuation mark after the closing quotation marks:

> Did Socrates say, "Know thyself"?
> He actually told me, "I don't have time for you"!

In the rare instance when a question mark or exclamation mark belongs both to the whole sentence and to the quoted part, use only one concluding mark and put it before the closing quotation marks:

> Did Socrates say, "What is truth?"

Reporting Tag at the End

If the quoted sentence would ordinarily end in a period, put a comma before the quotation marks:

> "I'm ready for you now," the director said.

Otherwise, use a question mark or exclamation mark as appropriate:

> "What do you have for me?" she asked.
> "Go away!" he yelled.

Reporting Tag in the Middle

If the reporting tag interrupts a sentence, set if off with commas:

"I hope," she said, "that we can still be friends."

If a complete sentence comes before the reporting tag, then put a period after the tag and capitalize the rest of the quoted material:

"Go away!" he yelled. "We don't want to see your ugly face around here anymore."

"What do you have for me?" she asked. "Is it a present?"

If the reporting tag is placed between two independent clauses that are separated by a semicolon, the semicolon follows the tag:

"Shakespeare wrote for the medium of his day," says Randall Jarrell; "if Shakespeare were alive now, he'd be writing *My Fair Lady*."

Punctuating Dialogue

When you are writing dialogue or reporting a conversation, you should start a new paragraph when there is a change in speaker, no matter how brief the quoted remarks may be:

"I saw you listening to those two little creeps," she hissed. "Were they talking about me?"

"I don't know," I said.

"You don't know! Why not?"

"They were speaking in Spanish."

Chapter 6
Mechanics

Many practices of written English are not strictly related to grammar. They are mechanical conventions that readers and writers recognize and accept. The mechanics of using capital letters, writing numbers and abbreviations, underlining and dividing words, and preparing a paper for submission for publication are all conventions that you have to follow if you want your writing to be acceptable to most readers.

6.A USING CAPITAL LETTERS

Before the invention of movable type, all letters were written as capitals. But the development of the printing press brought a system of using capital letters to signal the beginning of a sentence and to mark any word that the printer thought important. Today, the conventions of capitalization are fairly well settled and not too difficult to follow. There are five basic rules to keep in mind.

1. Capitalize the first word of a sentence.

The temperature dropped below zero again last night.
When is this cold snap supposed to end?
Bundle up before you go out!

If you quote a full sentence, capitalize the first word in that sentence, too, unless it is blended into the sentence that introduces it:

> In his essay on punctuation Lewis Thomas writes, "The commas are the most useful and usable of all the stops."
> It is Thomas's opinion that "exclamation points are the most irritating of all."

Capitalizing a sentence after a colon is optional:

> Dr. Thomas has a fondness for semicolons: they [*or* They] indicate that something more is coming.

2. Capitalize proper nouns and proper adjectives.

Proper nouns name specific people, places, and things (see Focus 6.1). Nouns that name general classes of people, places, and things are called **common nouns** and are not usually capitalized. *Proper adjectives* are formed from some proper nouns.

Common noun	Proper noun	Proper adjective
student	Juanita Sanchez	
country	Ireland	Irish
lover	Bill	
philosopher	Aristotle	Aristotelian

Focus 6.1

USAGE NOTE: WHAT NOUNS DO I CAPITALIZE?

The following are some categories of **proper nouns** that are usually capitalized. Many **common nouns** (such as *city*, *river*, *club*) are capitalized when used as part of a proper noun.

Specific Individuals

Katherine Hepburn	Jim McMahon	Alice Walker
Louis L'Amour	Oscar de la Renta	Flannery O'Connor

Focus 6.1 (continued)

Specific Places and Geographical Areas

Central America   Atlantic Ocean   New York City
the Andes Mountains   the Red River   the Southwest

[But: ocean currents, mountain streams, the southwest area]

Institutions, Organizations, Government Departments

Blackburn College   the Red Cross   Postal Service
the Supreme Court   the Chicago Cubs   Rotary Club

[But: college course, court order, club rules]

Historical Events, Documents, and Periods

the Vietnam War   the Bill of Rights   the Middle Ages
the Peasants' Revolt   the Gilded Age   Magna Carta

[But: human rights, war criminals, popular revolt]

Days of the Week, Months, Holidays

Thursday   April   Yom Kippur   the Fourth of July

Religions and Sacred Terms

Islam, Moslems   Christianity, Christians   Allah
the Koran   Methodists, Baptists   Christ
the Inquisition   the Bible   Aphrodite

Races, Nationalities, and Languages

Chicano   Caucasians   Swahili
African-American   Arabs   German

[But: blacks, whites]

Trade Names

Chevrolet   Xerox   Reeboks
Pampers   Banana Republic   Zenith

Months, holidays, and days of the week are treated as proper nouns, but the names of the seasons are not:

> We take our vacation in spring, usually in May before the Memorial Day weekend.

School subjects are capitalized only if they are names of languages; names of particular courses are capitalized:

> You should sign up for physics, Russian, economics, modern dance, and Creative Writing II.

3. Capitalize people's titles when they come before a proper name but not when they follow.

Senator Paul Simon	Paul Simon, a senator
Professor Anne Zahlan	Anne Zahlan, my professor

When titles are used without a name attached, they are usually not capitalized:

> The judge admonished the district attorney.

The exceptions to this rule involve the titles of very important public officials:

> The President sent a memo to the Attorney General.

4. Capitalize most words in the titles of books, articles, plays, films, songs, stories, poems, essays, paintings, and other such works.

> Huckleberry Finn
> Our Town
> "Dieting Can Be Fun"
> "My Baby Loves Love"

Articles (*a*, *an*, *the*) and **prepositions** and **conjunctions** of fewer than five letters are not capitalized unless they are the first or last word in a title or subtitle.

> Gone with the Wind
> The Fall of the City
> "Dieting Is a Waste of Time"
> "To My Dear and Loving Husband"

5. Capitalize the pronoun *I* and the interjection *O*.

> I did not know that I had so much to do.
> Hear our prayer, O Lord.

O is used primarily in religious and poetic invocations:

> "O, unspeakable passionate love."
>
> —Walt Whitman

Oh can stand alone or as part of a sentence to indicate strong emotions or a reflective pause:

> Oh, how I hate these early classes!
> Oh, I see. That's what you mean.

Oh is capitalized only when it is the first word of a sentence:

> I took an eight o'clock class, and, oh, how I regret it!

6.B   USING ABBREVIATIONS

Abbreviations are convenient and efficient; they can cut down on extra words. But abbreviations that are not familiar to your readers will cause confusion. If you are in doubt about using an abbreviation, spell the words out—at least the first time you use it.

Commonly Accepted Abbreviations

Personal and professional titles are usually abbreviated when they come immediately before or after proper names.

Titles Before Proper Names	Titles After Proper Names
Mr. William Vincent	William Vincent, Sr.
Ms. Carolyn Treadwell	Nicholas Blakely, Jr.
Mrs. David Radavich	Esther Blodgett, Ph.D.
Dr. Linda Coleman	Linda Coleman, M.D.
The Rev. Jesse Jackson	Edwina Newman, M.A.
St. Matthew	Mark Silverstein, LL.D.
Prof. Jeanne Simpson	Julio Juarez, D.D.S.

The abbreviations for academic degrees—*Ph.D.*, *M.A.*, *A.B.*, and the like—may be used without a name:

It took my brother ten years to complete his Ph.D.

But other titles should be spelled out if they are not used with a proper name:

My botany <u>professor</u> corrected the grammar on my paper.
Ali went to see his family <u>doctor</u> yesterday.

You should also avoid using redundant titles, such as *Dr. Jeremy Polk, M.D.* Choose one title or the other: *Dr. Jeremy Polk* or *Jeremy Polk, M.D.*

Familiar abbreviations for the names of organizations, agencies, corporations, countries, and famous people are acceptable in most writing situations:

Organizations   YMCA, NAACP, NOW, AFL-CIO
Agencies   IRS, FBI, CIA
Corporations   IBM, NBC, UPI
Countries   USA (or U.S.A.), USSR (or U.S.S.R.)
Famous people   JFK, LBJ, FDR

The abbreviations B.C., A.D., A.M. (or a.m.), P.M. (or p.m.), No. (or no.) and the symbol $ are acceptable when used with specific dates or numbers:

```
96 B.C. (follows the date)
A.D. 49 (precedes the date)
9:15 p.m.
$625
no. 24
```

Abbreviating Less Familiar Words

If you use a name or term frequently in a piece of writing, its abbreviation can cut down on unnecessary and cumbersome words. Give the full name or term the first time you use it, put its abbreviation in parentheses, and then use the abbreviation from then on:

```
The disease is caused by the human immunodefi-
ciency virus (HIV). Infected people may harbor HIV
in their bodies for several years before developing
symptoms.
```

But if you use the term only a few times, the abbreviation won't save much space and could be confusing to your readers. In that case spell the term out every time you use it.

Avoiding Inappropriate Abbreviations

Some familiar abbreviations are acceptable only in personal or informal writing. You should avoid abbreviating the following items in formal or academic writing:

Personal names   William, Elizabeth (not Wm., Eliz.)
Units of measurement   inches, pound (not in., lb.)
Days and months   Monday, August (not Mon., Aug.)
Courses of study   economics, history (not econ., hist.)
Divisions of written works   page, volume (not p., vol.)
Geographical names   Illinois, New Zealand (not IL, N.Z.)

You should not abbreviate *Company*, *Incorporated*, or *Brothers* unless their abbreviated forms are part of an official name.

In general, you should avoid the following Latin abbreviations except when citing sources or making parenthetical remarks:

cf.	compare (*confer*)
e.g.	for example (*exempli grata*)
etc.	and so forth (*et cetera*)
et al.	and others (*et alii*)
i.e.	that is (*id est*)
N.B.	note well (*nota bene*)

Focus 6.2

WRITING TIP: HOW DO I WRITE NUMBERS?

■ The decision to use figures or to write numbers out depends on the context. Figures are preferred in scientific and technical writing. In less specialized writing, numbers are usually spelled out. The following conventions apply to general writing.

■ Spell out numbers that can be written as one or two words:

During the Iran-Iraq war forty-one countries supplied the two sides with arms; twenty-eight supplied both sides.

■ Use figures for numbers that require more than two words to write out:

The war was militarily inconclusive, but the human toll was staggering: 450,000 dead and 800,000 wounded.

■ If you express one number in figures, write other numbers in the same sentence the same way:

Only 5 of the 217 casualties could have been avoided.

Focus 6.2 (continued)

- Spell out numbers that begin sentences, or rewrite the sentence:

  One thousand seventy-seven toxic waste sites have been targeted for cleanup.

  The EPA has targeted 1,077 toxic waste sites for cleanup.

- Use figures to express these items:

  Dates   November 4, 1937   350 B.C.   A.D. 85
  Addresses   711 Dover Avenue   210 East 35th Street
  Divisions of books   Chapter 9, page 218   volume 12
  Divisions of plays   Act IV, scene ii (or Act 4, scene 2)
  Percentages   78% (or 78 percent)
  Decimals, fractions   54.65 $12\frac{1}{4}$
  Scores and statistics   5-3   11 to 4   an average of 19
  Exact amounts of money $8,354 $5.4 million
  Time of day   5:00 a.m.   3:45 p.m.

  If not using a.m. or p.m., write out the time in words:

  five in the morning, twelve noon, six o'clock

6.C   USING ITALICS (UNDERLINING)

Italic type slants upward to the right. We use *italics* to set off words and phrases for emphasis or special consideration. Some word processors and printers can produce italic type. In handwritten or typed papers, you should underline material that would be italicized if set in type.

Italicizing Titles and Names

We generally italicize (or underline) the titles of long or complete works, such as books, plays, films, long poems, musical compositions, works of art, magazines, newspapers, and television and radio programs (see Focus 6.3). We also italicize (underline) the names of ships (the *Titanic*), aircraft (*Spirit of St. Louis*), spacecraft (*Apollo V*), and trains (the *Empire Builder*).

Focus 6.3

USAGE NOTE: WHAT TITLES DO I ITALICIZE?

Italicize (or underline) the titles of the following works and publications:

Books

The Grapes of Wrath
Teacher, Anne Sullivan

Plays

The Glass Menagerie
A Midsummer Night's Dream

Long Musical Works

Gershwin's *Rhapsody in Blue*
the Beatles' *Abbey Road*

Television and Radio Programs

Designing Women
All Things Considered

Long Poems

The Odyssey
In Memoriam

Films

Platoon
Citizen Kane

Paintings and Sculptures

O'Keefe's *Red Poppy No. VI*
the *Mona Lisa*

Magazines and Newspapers

the *St. Louis Post Dispatch*
the *New Yorker*

Note: An initial *the* in titles of magazines and newspapers is neither italicized nor capitalized, even if it is part of the official name.

The titles of sacred books, such as the Bible or the Koran, and of public documents, such as the Bill of Rights or the Constitution, are not italicized or underlined. The titles of shorter works—such as poems, short stories, songs, and essays—are enclosed in quotation marks: "My Last Duchess,"

"Good Country People," "Dancing in the Dark," "On Keeping a Notebook." The same is true for sections of works, such as chapter titles ("The Rise of the Middle Class") or titles of magazine articles ("An Interview with Jessica Lange").

Italicizing Words and Phrases

We italicize (underline) foreign words and phrases that have not yet been adopted into English:

> Standing en pointe is useful only if the candy bars are on the top shelf.

Words and phrases used so frequently that they become part of the English language—for example, pasta, bon voyage, and karate—do not need to be italicized or underlined. Most dictionaries will tell you whether the words you want to use should be italicized (underlined).

We also italicize or underline words, letters, or numbers referred to as words:

> In current usage, the pronouns he, him, and his outnumber she, her, and hers by a ratio of 4 to 1.

> Some people have trouble pronouncing the letter r, especially when it follows an i or an a.

Using Italics for Emphasis

Italics (underlining) can add emphasis to written language:

> We want our freedom today, not tomorrow.

This means of adding emphasis is obvious and easy to overdo. Creating emphasis through sentence structure and word choice is usually more effective.

6.D   DIVIDING WORDS

You would do better not to divide words at the end of a line, but if you must, remember to divide the word between syllables and use a hyphen to indicate the break. You should place the hyphen after the first part of the divided word, not at the beginning of the next line.

If you have some question about where the syllables in a word occur, consult a dictionary. Most dictionaries use dots to indicate the breaks between syllables in a word: di · a · lect, syl · la · ble, psy · chi · a · try.

Not all syllable breaks are appropriate for dividing words at the end of a line. The following rules will help you decide when and how to divide words.

1.   Do not divide words pronounced as one syllable.

[nonstandard]   The swimmers raced three leng-
                  ths of the pool.
[standard]   The swimmers raced three
                  lengths of the pool.

2.   Do not leave a single letter at the end of a line or begin a line with fewer than three letters.

[nonstandard]   The coach thought we couldn't get e-
                  nough practice before the big game.
[standard]   The coach thought we couldn't get
                  enough practice before the big game.

[nonstandard]   Parents should get to know each teach-
                  er in the school.
[standard]   Parents should get to know each
                  teacher in the school.

3.   Divide compound words between the words that form the compound.

Compound words are made up of two or more smaller words (homework, handwriting), and sometimes the component parts are separated by a hyphen (long-suffering, good-natured). You should break compound words only between the component parts or where the hyphen already occurs; other breaks will be confusing.

[confusing]   homecom-ing   self-reli-ant   mas-termind
[clear]   home-coming   self-reliant   master-mind

6.E   PREPARING A MANUSCRIPT

You want your papers to be legible, attractive, and consistent in format. The following guidelines will help you fulfill your reader's expectations about how a paper should look. These are standard guidelines, but your anticipated reader may want you to follow other conventions—be sure to check with that person.

Choosing Appropriate Materials

For Typed Papers

- Use $8\frac{1}{2} \times 11$ inch, 20-pound paper. Avoid erasable paper: ink smears easily on the coated surface.
- Type on only one side of a sheet and double-space.
- Use a fresh black ribbon.
- Use a liquid correction fluid to make corrections; do not strike over or use Xs or hyphens to cross out mistakes.
- For a paper typed on a word processor, be sure the print quality is easy to read. Tell the printer to double strike, if possible. Separate the pages of a continuous sheet, remove the feeder strips, assemble the pages in order, and fasten with a paper clip or staple.

For Handwritten Papers

- Make sure that handwritten submissions are acceptable.
- Use $8\frac{1}{2} \times 11$ inch, wide-ruled, white paper; do not use legal-size paper or sheets torn from a notebook.
- Write on only one side of a sheet; write on every other line to increase legibility.
- Use blue or black ink, not pencil.
- Use an ink eraser or correction fluid to make corrections; do not scribble over or black out a mistake.

Following Standard Format

Margins and Indention

- Leave about an inch and a half for the margins at the left and top of each page; leave one-inch margins at the right and bottom.

- Indent the first line of each paragraph five spaces (a half an inch in handwriting and computer printing) from the left margin.

Pagination

- Number all pages in the upper right-hand corner of the page, one-half inch from the top and aligned with the right margin.
- Number all pages after the first page: count the first page, but do not put a number on it.
- Use arabic numerals (2, 3, and so on); do not put a period after the number and do not enclose the number in parentheses or hyphens.

Punctuation and Typing

- In typing, leave one space between words and after commas, semicolons, and colons.
- Leave two spaces after sentence periods, question marks, and exclamation points.
- Form a dash by typing two hyphens with no space between them; do not put a space between a word and a dash.

Proofreading

Your ideas deserve clear, correct expression. You should proofread your paper at least twice, looking for different kinds of errors each time. These suggestions for proofreading will increase your accuracy:

1. Read sentence by sentence from the bottom of the page to the top (to keep your attention focused on finding mistakes, not on content).
2. Read again, looking for any particular errors that you tend to make: fragments, comma splices, typical misspellings, and so on.

3. Go over each page using an index card with a small rect-
   angle cut in the middle. This technique will force you to
   look at only a few words at a time.
4. When in doubt about spelling or meaning, look words up
   in a dictionary. If you are using a word processor, do not
   forget to use the spelling check.
5. Get a reliable friend to check your work one more time.

Appendix A
Principal Parts
of Irregular Verbs

Present	Past	Past participle
am/is/are	was/were	been
arise	arose	arisen
awake	awoke	awaked
bear	bore	borne or born
beat	beat	beaten
become	became	become
begin	began	begun
bend	bent	bent
bite	bit	bitten or bit
bleed	bled	bled
blow	blew	blown
break	broke	broken
bring	brought	brought
build	built	built
burst	burst	burst
buy	bought	bought
cast	cast	cast
catch	caught	caught
choose	chose	chosen
cling	clung	clung
come	came	come
creep	crept	crept
deal	dealt	dealt
dig	dug	dug
dive	dived or dove	dived
do, does	did	done

Present	Past	Past participle
drag[1]	dragged	dragged
draw	drew	drawn
dream	dreamed or dreamt	dreamed or dreamt
drink	drank	drunk
drive	drove	driven
drown[2]	drowned	drowned
eat	ate	eaten
fall	fell	fallen
fight	fought	fought
find	found	found
fly	flew	flown
forget	forgot	forgotten or forgot
freeze	froze	frozen
get	got	gotten or got
give	gave	given
go, goes	went	gone
grow	grew	grown
hang (suspend)	hung	hung
hang (execute)[3]	hanged	hanged
have	had	had
hear	heard	heard
hide	hid	hidden
hold	held	held
hurt	hurt	hurt
keep	kept	kept
kneel	knelt or kneeled	knelt or kneeled
know	knew	known
lay (put)	laid	laid
lead	led	led
leap	leapt or leaped	leapt or leaped
let (allow)	let	let
lie (recline)	lay	lain
lighted	lit or lighted	lit or lighted
lose	lost	lost
make	made	made
pay	paid	paid

[1] Not irregular, but often misused (*drug* instead of *dragged*).
[2] Not irregular, but often misused (*drownded* instead of *drowned*).
[3] Not irregular, but often misused (*hung* instead of *hanged*).

Present	Past	Past participle
prove	proved	proved or proven
put	put	put
read	read	read
ride	rode	ridden
ring	rang	rung
rise	rose	risen
run	ran	run
say	said	said
see	saw	seen
seek	sought	sought
send	sent	sent
set	set	set
shake	shook	shaken
shine	shone	shone
shoot	shot	shot
show	showed	shown
shrink	shrank or shrunk	shrunk or shrunken
sing	sang or sung	sung
sink	sank or sunk	sunk
sit	sat	sat
slay	slew	slain
sleep	slept	slept
slink	slunk	slunk
sneak	sneaked or snuck[4]	sneaked or snuck
spay[5]	spayed	spayed
speak	spoke	spoken
spin	spun	spun
spring	sprang or sprung	sprung
stand	stood	stood
steal	stole	stolen
sting	stung	stung
strike	struck	struck or stricken
strive	strove or strived	striven or strived
swear	swore	sworn
swim	swam	swum
swing	swung	swung
take	took	taken

---

[4] Many authorities still consider *snuck* nonstandard, but this form seems to be preferred in speaking and informal writing.
[5] Not irregular, but often misused (*spaded* instead of *spayed*).

Present	Past	Past participle
teach	taught	taught
tear	tore	torn
throw	threw	thrown
wake	woke or waked	waked or woken
wear	wore	worn
weave	wove	woven
win	won	won
wind (wrap, twist)	wound	wound
wring	wrung	wrung
write	wrote	written

Appendix B
Tenses of Verbs

There are six main tenses in English.

Simple present   (base form, -s/-es added to third person singular)

I walk, she runs, they go

Used for actions happening at the moment, or for habitual, continuous, or characteristic actions.

Simple past   (base + -ed; irregular verbs vary)

I walked, he ran, they went

Used for actions completed at a definite past time.

Simple future   (will + base form)

I will walk, it will run, they will go

Used for actions that have not yet begun.

Present perfect   (have + past participle)

I have walked, she has run, they have gone

Used for actions completed at some unspecified time in the past or continuing into the present.

Past perfect   (*had* + past participle)

> I had walked, he had run, they had gone

> Used for actions that were completed before some other past action occurred: "The police <u>had</u> <u>arrested</u> Rupert by the time we arrived."

Future perfect   (*will have* + past participle)

> I will have walked, she will have run, they will have gone

> Used for actions that will be completed by or before some specified time in the future: "Your investment <u>will</u> <u>have</u> <u>doubled</u> in ten years."

Each of these six tenses has a *progressive* form (*be* + present participle) to indicate an ongoing action:

Present progressive:	I am walking.
Past progressive:	I was walking.
Future progressive:	I will be walking.
Present perfect progressive:	I have been walking.
Past perfect progressive:	I had been walking.
Future perfect progressive:	I will have been walking.

The present and past tenses also have an *emphatic* form (*do* + base form):

> I <u>do</u> <u>remember</u> your name.
> She <u>did</u> <u>go</u> to the wedding.

In addition, a variety of other auxiliaries (called *modals*) can be used to form verb strings with different senses of time and attitude: *I may go, I could go, I should go, I must go, I used to go, I ought to go, I can go,* and so forth.

Glossary of Grammatical Terms*

Active voice   A feature of transitive verbs that expresses an action initiated by the subject and directed toward an object: "The *batter* [subject] *hit* [verb] the ball [object]."

Adjective   A large class of words that act as noun modifiers; most can be inflected for degree (*strong, stronger, strongest*) and are often qualified or intensified (*rather strong, too strong*).

Adjective clause   A subordinate (or dependent) clause that modifies a noun or pronoun: "The book *that I lost* belonged to the school library." See also *relative clause.*

Adverb   A class of words that act as verb modifiers and sometimes modify adjectives and other adverbs, usually giving information about time, place, manner, and cause. Some adverbs have comparative and superlative forms (*more slowly, fastest*) and can be qualified (*very fast, rather slowly*). See also *flat adverb.*

Adverb clause   A subordinate (or dependent) clause that modifies a verb, adjective, adverb, or whole sentence: "We can go *as* soon *as the storm is over.*"

Adverbial conjunction   See *conjunctive adverb.*

* The abbreviation *q.v.* (Latin for "which see") directs the reader to glossary entries for terms that are used within definitions; *qq.v.* refers to several terms that are listed in the glossary.

Agreement The correspondence in number and person between a subject and its verb; the correspondence in number, person, case, and (sometimes) gender between a pronoun and its antecedent.

Antecedent The noun or nominal that a pronoun stands for and refers to.

Appositive A word or group of words, usually a noun phrase, that renames another noun or noun phrase: "Ginny, *my cousin*, was enjoying her favorite pastime—*watching soap operas*."

Auxiliary A verb marker (also called a *helping verb*) used with a main verb to indicate tense and (sometimes) voice, person, number, and mood. Auxiliaries include forms of *have*, *be*, and *do*, as well as the modals (*q.v.*), such as *will*, *may*, and *should*.

Balanced structure See *parallel structure*.

Base form The uninflected form of the verb, which in all cases except *be* is the present tense form: *eat*, *stop*. See also *infinitive*.

Being verb The most irregular verb in English, with eight forms: *be*, *am*, *is*, *are*, *was*, *were*, *been*, *being*. See also *linking verb*.

Broad reference Use of a pronoun such as *this*, *that*, *which*, or *such* to refer to a whole idea or statement, not to a single noun: "Jane has quit her job, *which* surprises me."

Case A feature of nouns and certain pronouns that shows relationship to other words. Personal pronouns—and the relative *who*—have three cases: subjective, objective, possessive. Nouns have only one case inflection: possessive; the case of nouns for all other uses is called *common case*. The pronouns *you* and *it* have only possessive (*your*, *its*) and common case.

Clause A group of words with a subject and a finite verb. See also *independent clause*, *dependent clause*, *relative clause*, and *subordinate clause*.

Coherence   The logical relationship among parts of a sentence, paragraph, or an entire discourse.

Collective noun   A noun that is singular in form but refers to a collection of individuals: *crowd, cast, family, jury, team.*

Comma blunder   See *comma splice.*

Comma fault   See *comma splice.*

Comma splice   A sentence boundary error in which two independent clauses are joined by a comma with no coordinating conjunction.

Common nouns   Words that name general classes of people, places, or things; usually not capitalized.

Comparative form   The form of an adjective or adverb that shows some increase in quality, quantity, or degree. *Larger* is the comparative of *large*; *more comfortable* is the comparative of *comfortable.*

Complement   A word or phrase added to a verb to complete the sense of a sentence. Direct objects and indirect objects are the complements for transitive verbs. Linking verbs are completed by predicate nominatives and predicate adjectives. See also *subjective complement.*

Complementation   The grammatical operation of completing a verb by adding objects or subjective complements.

Completer   Another term for a complement (*q.v.*).

Complex sentence   A sentence that includes at least one dependent clause.

Compound sentence   A sentence with two or more independent clauses.

Compound subject   Two or more nominals that function as the coordinate subject of a verb.

Confused sentence   See *mixed constructions.*

Conjunction A class of structure words that connect words, phrases, and sentences. Conjunctions can be divided into coordinating, correlative, subordinating, and adverbial (*qq.v.*).

Conjunctive adverb An adverb (such as *also*, *however*, *furthermore*, *therefore*) that connects two independent clauses. When a conjunctive adverb introduces a second independent clause, it must be preceded by a semicolon: "We had been told to stay inside; *moreover*, we were warned not to turn on any lights."

Coordinate Term applied to elements that are similar in grammatical construction.

Coordinating conjunction A connecting word that links two or more sentences or structures within a sentence as equals: *and*, *but*, *or*, *nor*, *yet*. *So* and *for* act as coordinating conjuctions only between independent clauses.

Correlative conjunction A two-part connective that links coordinate structures: *either . . . or*, *neither . . . nor*, *not only . . . but also*, *both . . . and*.

Dependent clause A clause that functions as an adjective, adverb, or nominal (noun). A dependent clause relies on an independent clause for its complete meaning.

Determiner A word that signals or marks a noun. Determiners include articles (*a*, *an*, *the*), numbers, possessives, demonstratives (*this*, *that*), and some indefinite pronouns (for example, *some*, *each*, *every*, *many*).

Direct object The noun or nominal that names the goal or receiver of the verb's action: "She ate *the pie*"; "I enjoy *reading long novels*."

Expletive A meaningless word (*there*, *it*) that enables a writer to emphasize the subject of a sentence by placing it after the verb (usually a being verb): "*There* is no reason to get upset"; "*It* is impossible to find a cab at this hour."

Faulty predication   A sentence construction in which the main parts (subject, verb, complement) do not fit together logically or grammatically.

Finite verb   A verb that indicates the main predication of an independent clause. A finite verb allows contrasts in tense and mood. All verb forms are finite except infinitives, participles, and gerunds.

Flat adverb   A subcategory of adverbs that can be used as adjectives without the addition of *-ly* or any other suffix: *fast, hard, late, high, long,* and so forth.

Fragment   A group of words that is punctuated as a sentence but lacks a subject or finite verb or begins with a subordinating word.

Fused sentence   See *run-on sentence.*

Gender   A feature of personal pronouns that divides them into masculine (*he/him*), feminine (*she/her*), and neuter (*it*). Some nouns also convey gender distinctions: *waiter/waitress, man/woman,* and so forth.

Gerund   A verb form ending in *-ing* and used as a nominal: "*Playing* chess requires concentration"; "I hate *washing* dishes."

Helping verb   See *auxiliary.*

Historical present   The stylistic use of the present tense to describe past events, especially in writing about literary works. Also called *literary present.*

Imperative   A type of sentence used to issue a command or directive. The imperative verb is in the base form, and the subject is usually not expressed (and is understood to be *you*): "Take off your hat."

Indefinite pronouns   A large group of pronouns that are used to refer to unspecified individuals or items: *one, any, somebody, several, each, everyone, none, anything, many, few, both, either,* and so forth.

Independent clause   The main clause of a sentence. It is grammatically and logically complete and can stand by itself as a sentence. See also *sentence*.

Indirect object   The noun or pronoun that tells who benefits from the action of the verb. In the sentence "She gave her students a tough assignment," the indirect object (*students*) names the recipient of the thing given, the direct object (*assignment*).

Infinitive   The base form of the verb, usually expressed with *to*: *to run*, *to be*, *to cheat*. Infinitives are verbals that can be used as adjectives, adverbs, or nominals. See also *perfect infinitive*.

Inflection   A change in the form of a word, usually the addition of an ending, to show a change in meaning or grammatical role.

Intensifier   See *qualifier*.

Interrupter   Nonessential words and phrases that interrupt the flow of a sentence. They are usually set off with commas: "Many people, for example, do not realize that ozone is a by-product of dry cleaning."

Intonation   The pattern of a spoken sentence, involving stress, pitch, and pauses.

Intransitive verb   An action verb that does not need a direct object to be complete: "The child *ran* into the street"; "She *jogs* every day for an hour."

Irregular verb   A verb that does *not* form its past tense and past participle by adding -*d* or -*ed* to the base form: *sing/sang/sung*; *think/thought/thought*. See Appendix A.

Linking verb   A verb that acts as a link between the subject and the subjective complement. Forms of *be* are the most common linking verbs; but *seem*, *become*, *appear*, and the verbs relating to the senses, such as *taste* or *look*, also function in this way.

Literary present   See *historical present*.

Mixed construction   A sentence that does not combine its main parts (subject, verb, completer) in a logical or grammatical way.

Modal auxiliary   Helping verbs that indicate such conditions as necessity, possibility, capability, and willingness: *can* write, *should* write, *may* write, *must* write, *would* write, and so forth.

Modifier   Any word or group of words that defines, qualifies, limits, or describes the meaning of another word or word group. Modifiers are either adjectives or adverbs, or phrases and clauses that act as adjectives and adverbs (*qq.v.*).

Mood   The quality of a verb that shows how the speaker or writer views the action expressed: as fact (indicative mood), as contrary to fact (subjunctive), or as a probability or possibility (conditional). See also *modal auxiliary.*

Nominal   Any structure that is used as a noun or noun phrase would be used—i.e., as subject, predicate nominative, direct object, indirect object, appositive, or object of a preposition (*qq.v.*).

Nonfinite verb   An "unfinished" verb form that cannot serve as a sentence verb; also called *verbal* (*gerund, participle,* or *infinitive*).

Nonrestrictive modifier   A phrase or clause that comments on a noun but does not define it. Nonrestrictive modifiers are set off with commas when they follow a noun: "Sleep, *which we all need*, occupies about one-third of our lives."

Nonstandard English   Any expression or usage that does not conform to the form approved by educated users of the language.

Noun   Traditionally defined as a word that names a person, place, thing, or idea. Nouns function as subjects, objects, and complements; most have plural and possessive inflections.

Noun clause   A subordinate (dependent) clause that fills any of the roles of a noun or noun phrase: *"Whoever was driving* [subject] should be ticketed."

Noun phrase   A noun with all its attendant determiners and modifiers: "an old iron bucket."

Number   A feature of nouns, pronouns, and verbs that shows singular or plural meaning.

Objective case   The form of personal pronouns (*me, her, them*) and the relative *who* (*whom*) that is used when these pronouns function as objects (direct object, indirect object, object of a preposition).

Parallel structure   The technique of expressing all coordinate parts of a sentence in the same grammatical form.

Participle   The verb forms that can be used as adjectives. See *present participle* and *past participle*.

Parts of speech   The grammatical categories into which words are traditionally grouped according to form, function, and meaning: nouns, pronouns, verbs, adjectives, adverbs, prepositions, conjunctions, and interjections.

Passive voice   A feature of transitive-verb sentences in which the subject is acted upon: "The ball *was hit* by the batter." Passive verbs are formed by combining a *be* auxiliary with a past participle: *is seen, were given, will be used.*

Past participle   The third principal part of a verb, usually ending in *-d, -ed, -t, -en,* or *-n.* The past participle is used as an adjective (the *driven* snow) as well as in forming the perfect tenses (*has driven, had driven*) and the passive voice (*was driven*).

Perfect infinitive   The infinitive marker *to* + the base form of *have* + a past participle: *to have seen.*

Person   The form of a personal pronoun that distinguishes the speaker or writer (first person), the person spoken to (second person), and the person or thing spoken about (third person). Verbs indicate person in one instance: adding -s to the third person singular of the present tense: he *sings*.

Personal pronoun   Those pronouns that show grammatical person, as well as case, number, and gender: *I*, *you*, *he*, *she*, *it*, *we*, *they* (the subjective forms).

Phrase   A group of related words that does not contain a predication (subject + verb).

Positive form   The noncomparative form of an adjective or adverb. The positive form of "prettiest" is "pretty."

Possessive   The inflected form of nouns (*the dancer's*, *Mitch's*) and pronouns (*my*, *our*, *his*, *her*, *theirs*, and so forth) that usually shows ownership, although the meaning of the possessive can also convey measurement (a *penny's* worth), origin (*their* suggestion), and simple description (*today's* catch).

Predicate   The part of the sentence other than the subject and its modifiers. A predicate contains a finite verb and may include modifiers and complements.

Predicate adjective   An adjective that completes a linking verb and modifies the subject: "The fur feels *soft*"; "The corn is *green*."

Predicate nominative   A nominal that completes a linking verb and renames or identifies the subject: "That man is *my neighbor*"; "His hobby is *collecting stamps*."

Predication   The grammatical process of combining a subject with a verb to create a statement or express an idea.

Preposition   A structure word that links a nominal to another part of the sentence: "If Tim doesn't hear *from* Gary *by* noon, he will call Lisa *for* a ride." Prepositions may consist of more than one word: *according to*, *because of*, *out of*.

Prepositional phrase A group of words that begins with a preposition and ends with its object (a nominal): *under the table*, *after waiting an hour*.

Present participle The *-ing* form of a verb, used to make progressive verbs (We *are driving* to town) and to modify nominals (a *driving* rain).

Principal parts The three forms of a verb that are used to make tenses: base form (*drive*, *stop*), past tense (*drove*, *stopped*), past participle (*driven*, *stopped*).

Pronoun A word that substitutes for a noun (or any nominal). There are several types of pronouns, the most common being *personal*, *relative*, and *indefinite* (*qq.v.*).

Proper nouns Words that name specific persons, places, or things; usually capitalized.

Qualifier A word that limits or intensifies the meaning of an adjective or adverb: "She talked *rather* slowly"; "They look *extremely* happy."

Reference The feature of a pronoun that relates it to an antecedent (the noun it stands for). Reference is controlled by number, person, case, and gender.

Regular verb A verb that forms its past tense and past participle by adding *-d* or *-ed* to the base form: *talk/talked/talked*.

Relative clause A dependent clause that modifies a noun and is introduced by a relative pronoun (*who*, *which*, *that*), or sometimes by an adverb (*when*, *where*, *why*); an adjective clause (*q.v.*).

Relative pronoun The pronouns *who*, *which*, and *that* in their roles as introducers of a relative (adjective) clause (*q.v.*).

Restrictive modifier A phrase or clause that limits or identifies the noun it modifies: "The man *who called last night* is interested in your car." A restrictive modifier is not set off with commas.

Run-on sentence   Two independent clauses that have been run together without punctuation or a connecting word. Also called a *fused sentence*.

Sentence   A group of related words containing a subject and a finite verb and not introduced by a subordinating word.

Standard written English   Language usage that conforms to the widely accepted norm for the edited public writing found in newspapers, magazines, and books.

Structure word   Any one of several classes of words, such as prepositions, conjunctions, determiners, and expletives, that mark and make clear the grammatical relationships in a sentence.

Subject   The noun or nominal that is the agent (or topic) of the action (or state) expressed by the finite verb in a sentence or clause.

Subjective case   The form for personal pronouns (and the relative pronoun *who*) when they function as the subject or the subjective complement.

Subjective complement   The nominal or adjective that follows a linking verb and renames or modifies the subject of the sentence. Also called *predicate nominative* and *predicate adjective (qq.v.)*.

Subordinate clause   A dependent clause introduced by a subordinating word, such as *if, since, because, that, although*. Subordinate clauses can be further described as *relative clauses, adjective clauses, adverb clauses,* and *noun clauses (qq.v.)*.

Subordinating conjunction/word   The word or phrase that begins a dependent clause and links it to an independent clause: "She studies *while* her laundry is in the dryer." Also called a *subordinator*.

Superlative form   The form of an adjective or adverb expressing the highest degree of comparison. "Largest" is the superlative form of "large"; "most carefully" is the superlative of "carefully."

Syntax   The way in which words are combined to form phrases, clauses, and sentences; the relationship of sentence parts to one another.

Tense   The feature of verbs and auxiliaries that indicates time: past, present, and future are the basic time indications for verbs in English. See Appendix B.

Transitive verb   A verb that expresses an action and requires at least one complement, the direct object, to be grammatically complete. With very few exceptions, transitive verbs are those that can be transformed into the passive voice.

Verb   A word or string of words that indicates the action or state of being of a subject. Every verb, without exception, has an *-s* and an *-ing* form; every verb also has a past tense and a past participle, although these vary a good deal with irregular verbs; and all verbs, without exception, can be combined with auxiliaries.

Verbal   The present participle, past participle, and infinitive forms of a verb, used as modifiers or as nominals (nouns). Like finite verbs, verbals may have complements, modifiers, and (sometimes) subjects, but they do not function as main verbs for clauses or sentences.

Voice   The term that describes the relationship between the subject and the verb: either *active voice* or *passive voice* (*qq.v.*).

Index